Rebel Rhymes

Volume 2

By
Tony Tobin.

Foreword by Ken Tobin.

ISBN: 9798868057441

In memory of two stalwarts of Cork City FC.
Gone but never forgotten - my uncle,
Finbarr O' Shea and my dear
friend John F. Kennedy.

"Your City, Your Club."

Contents

Foreword

I think it's safe to say that I know my brother well and I think it's also safe to say it comes as no surprise to see a second Rebel Rhymes book of poetry from Tony.

Our family has a passion for sport, but even more so for Cork City Football Club and we have all been fans of the club since its inception back in 1984.

We would all have great memories of coming home after a game and our late father Noel waiting to hear how the lads got on, who scored and who played well.

It's a Tobin tradition that is carried on to this day by our mother Margaret (Nana Mar), now in her 80s, and as keen as any Tobin on how the latest City game has gone. But it is Tony by far who has the greatest passion and love for the club, and it shows in many ways - from his trips to the club shop to check out the latest club merchandise, to being a season ticket holder, all those photographs, not missing a game and of course his love for the club with brilliantly written poems about every aspect of his beloved Cork City FC.

Poems about the famous 'Shed End' and the Rebel Army fans that reside there, to those who have graced Turners Cross past and present. From the late Aoife Linehan, Uncle Finbar, Noelle, the legend Liam Miller and club greats like Colin Healy, Johnny C and Sean Maguire (who once informed me he has his poem framed and proudly hanging in his home in England!).

Tony is surrounded by a loving family including his wife Carol, four sons and his grandchildren who are so proud of him and what he has achieved not only with these two books of poetry, but as a husband, father, and Granddad. I know I can say on behalf of myself, our brother Alan, sisters Tina, Lucy, Ber and our mother that we love and are so proud of our big brother.

Best of luck to you, Tony with the new book of poetry. Happy reading and thank you to all who buy and support it. CCFC 'til I die!

Your proud brother,

Ken Tobin.

1920 The Fight for Freedom

It's the year 1920, the mood is quite tense,
The people scrape by, on just a few pence.
The IRA are in a dog fight, to the bitter end,
For God and Ireland, and their families to defend.
Whatever you inflict on me and mine,
In Rebel Cork we don't toe the line.
You killed MacCurtain, with children crying,
In front of his wife, you left him dying.
Shot down like a dog, to Britain's shame,
For the crime of being Irish, representing Sinn Féin.

The Irish people are donning the green,
No more bending the knee, to an English Queen.
Terence MacSwiney was the new Lord Mayor,
A proud Irishman, who showed no fear.
An IRA leader, he marched in formation,
Arrested by the Crown, on a charge of sedation.
He was sent to prison, to his local Cork Gaol,
Those who suffer the most, will always prevail.
Wise words, from a very wise man,
Standing up for his people, whenever he can.

The men are on hunger strike, for a noble cause,
Not a morsel of food, will pass through their jaws.
After 67 days Michael Fitzgerald would die,
Another martyr for Ireland, was the battle cry.
Joe Murphy was next to pass away,
Ensuring that Ireland, would have her day.
They had moved MacSwiney to Brixton Gaol,
True to the cause, he was now very frail.
The world was watching, sending their prayers,
To the people of Cork, who had lost two Lord Mayors.

Tom Barry's flying column, in West Cork had made plans,
They won a fierce battle, in Killmichael against the Tans.
Gandhi and Mandela, who also fought for freedom,
Told those who would listen, that MacSwiney, had inspired them.

Men went to work, on the banks of the Lee,
Some not returning that day for their tea.
Faceless soldiers, Black and Tans with no names,
Rampaging through the city, Cork was in flames.
The Government in London, had finally realised,
That the Irish people, had won the prize.
The news they had dreamed of, they would soon receive,
The British had decided, it was time to leave.
The War of Independence, had restored the nation's faith,
With the birth of a nation, the Irish Free State.

One hundred years, have passed us by,
Does anyone care, I'd say no, I won't lie.
Where's the statues, for us to remember,
Our two Lord Mayors, that wouldn't surrender.
They gave their lives, for the Irish cause,
So the people of Ireland, could make their own laws.
The least we could do, is build statues of stone,
In Cork City centre, the place they called home.
Each year we could visit, to give them our thanks,
With a fresh bunch of flowers, and a verse of the Banks.

A City Rising

A season to forget, bar our brave defenders,
And fans buying chips, from the Young Offenders.
Caulfield left the scene, our best ever boss,
Agree or not, he was a huge loss.
A trophy-less season, for us on Leeside,
Nothing to play for, but the shirt, and our pride.
We couldn't score a goal, not even a spotter,
Another boss gone, goodbye John Cotter.
Neale Fenn came in, but couldn't stop the rot,
Loss after loss, that was our lot.
Try as we could, we just weren't able,
Fighting for our lives, at the foot of the table.

Some legends made way, like Benno and Mark,
The boss lit a fuse, looking for a spark.
It didn't stop the tide, but at least he was trying,
He found a gem, our new keeper Tadhg Ryan.
Marky Sull was dropped too, to a man very harsh,
But we found another gem, in Beineón O'Brien-Whitmarsh.

It's not so bad, as it first might seem,
It takes a long time, to build a new team.
The first thing to sort, is the central spine,
From stopping the goals, to a top number nine.
We have Tadhg in goal, McCarthy at the back,
McCormack the enforcer, Beineón in attack.
Buckley and Morrissey, and O'Connor out wide,
Alec Byrne in the centre, who seems to glide.
Griffin and Hurley, and Bargary too,
Crowley and Murphy, to name just a few.

Roll on next season, new memories to be made,
For we are Cork City, we won't stay in the shade.
We'll support our players, get it down and play ball,
Sing up the Rebel Army, we're together after all.
Back at the top, that may sound surprising,
Is there anything more glorious than a city rising?

A Horrible Year

Goodbye 2020, a horrible year,
Most of the world, was gripped by fear.
Coronavirus arrived at our door,
Shook our foundations, to its very core.
It picked out the weak, the vulnerable, the old,
Some called it a hoax, it's just like a cold,
Tell that to the families, with no one to hold.

It's you not the virus,
That's cruel and cold.
A bedside locker, empty and bare,
At the breakfast table, there's an empty chair.
Scientists warned, a virus would come round,
We weren't ready, no masks to be found.
We vote for these people, to protect us from harm,
But they're full of hot air, when they turn on the charm.

A Turkish immigrant, gathered round him, a team,
Worked day and night to produce a vaccine.
They did all the tests, they did all the trials,
It's a race against time, to make millions of vials.
The virus is rampant, the medics can't cope,
Vaccinate the people, It's our only hope.
We hope and pray, it will lift the fear,
So that 2021, is a much better year.

A Large Ninety-Nine

Summer days, and the weather's fine,
A trip to the beach, and a Ninety-Nine.
There's nothing more Irish, on the way back home,
To stop at Centra, for a Ninety-Nine Cone.

Some are small, some are quite tall,
Just ask the assistant, it's always your call.
Some would say I'm like a dog with a bone,
More often than not, I'm holding a cone.

If you don't eat that flake, you think you will burst,
But have a good lick, of the ice-cream first.
From West Cork to East Cork, the choice is amazing,
At the side of the road, while watching cows grazing.

Drive to Clonakilty, then onto Skibbereen,
The beaches are gorgeous, the Ninety-Nines are supreme.
Over to Barleycove, and then the Mizen Head,
Instead of a coffee, have a Ninety-Nine instead.

Over to East Cork, to the beach at Garryvoe,
Where the ice-cream machine, is always set to flow.
Move onto Killeagh, for a coffee to go,
Then onto Youghal, the star of the show.

When the Sun is shining, Youghal is divine,
No better place for a large Ninety-Nine.
When you're feeling full, don't sit and talk,
Head out on the boardwalk, for a nice brisk walk.

Pack up the car, it's time to head home,
Stop off in Castlemartyr, for an ice-cream cone.
After a long old day, at last it's bedtime,
I wish you sweet dreams, of a large Ninety-Nine.

A Refugee's Plight

Eeny meeny miny moe,
No room at the inn, so off you go.
No room for you, In this safe place,
Because of the colour, of your face.
Dirty, frail, and very thin,
Their only crime, the wrong colour skin.
Fleeing wars in the Middle East,
While drones drop bombs, on their wedding feast.
Innocent children left for dead,
Presumed safe, asleep in bed.
Bombed by the west, and the east gets no pass,
Betrayed by our government, with poison gas.
We make it to west, to find new homes,
We need some help, to repair our bones.
You're welcome here, you are our brothers,
But a wall of fires, are set by others.
What did we do, to deserve this plight,
Caught in the middle, of another man's fight.
Our country's rich, because of oil,
Buried deep beneath the soil.
Not for us the finest things,
The sole preserve, of princes and kings.
If you could let us, stay for a while,
To regain our strength, to see our kids smile.
When the fighting stops, and our land is free,
From invading forces, and tyranny.
We'll pack our bags, we'll shake your hand,
And return, once more, to our own homeland.
We thank you Ireland, for taking us in,
My family and I, and even our kin.
We're back now, where we want to be,
By a warm sun, and Mediterranean Sea.
Governments of the world, rein yourselves in,
Leave us alone, and let us begin.
To build our homes, and dream once more,
To live and love, like we did before.

A Robin's Feather

A feather floated by today,
With a message from my dad to say.
Don't be down, don't be sad,
Such a full and happy life I had.
I had seven children, with my wonderful wife,
The greatest achievement, in all my life.

For fifty years, I worked hard at my job,
Came out the other side, with the help of God.
Went back to school, and earned the right,
To help my neighbours, stand up and fight.
I met a friend throwing bowls on a mat,
Remained friends for life, I was happy with that.

We travelled the world, from China to Youghal,
We laughed every day, we had a ball.
It came to an end, like all things do,
My 92 years, like a bird they flew.
I promise you all, you'll stay in my prayers,
Until the day you climb those stairs.

Live your life, with gusto and a smile,
Don't settle for an inch, go the whole mile.
For if you do, I promise you this,
A happy life, a life of bliss.
If you meet a robin, that's unusually tame,
Have a little chat, and say my name.
Don't feel stupid, don't feel bad,
For the robin brings greetings, of happiness from Dad.

All We Need Is Fenn

A cockney boy, from London town,
He was here before, he had a shop in town.
He won us a title in 2005,
When Neale had the ball, the Cross came alive.
He was so good, to his foes he was a pain,
Had a touch and a pass, just like Patsy Freyne.

Two seasons ago, we were flying high,
On top of the world, we could touch the sky.
But we lost our way, we dropped like a stone,
We cut back on the staff, pared back to the bone.

Some fans stopped going, only die-hards at the Cross,
So the board called a meeting, to find a new boss.
We need to do something, we owe it to the fans,
It was an all-nighter, ordered chips and a bag of cans.

Let's trawl the country, to find a new man,
To get us playing football, and see if we can.
Get back to two years ago, cause we were champions back then,
It was staring us in the face, all we need is Fenn.

Lets fill the Cross, for Neale's first game,
Let our rivals know, they're in the house of pain.
Get all four stands to shout out his name,
Then I have no doubt, we'll win the game.
For this is now, forget about back then,
Let's all sing together, all we need is Fenn.

All You Need Is Love

A special couple, got engaged today,
Kim and Stephen, hip hip hooray.
A nicer couple you couldn't meet,
Their search for a soulmate, is now complete.

Looking forward now, to their wedding day,
To proclaim their love, and together they'll stay.
Kim is a lasher, Stephen is cool,
A singer of songs, on a three-legged stool.

I think they'll be grand, I think they'll be fine,
A great start to their life, down in Carrigaline.
Stephen writes music, and beautiful songs,
A great man for the sessions, and the best singsongs.

Kim's a great person, it was angels that brought her,
She's a part of our family, just like our daughter.
Cupid is right, he knows who to choose,
Any day now, we're expecting some news.

We wish you good luck, nothing bad at your door,
All you need is love, nothing less, nothing more.

Baby Shay

He's here he's here, he arrived today,
Our bundle of joy, our Baby Shay.
Ten fingers ten toes, two ears and a nose,
All in their place, and boy does it show.

He looks like his Dad, and Mother as well
You can see when he smiles, it's easy to tell.
He loves his books, his interests are many,
But his favourite time is on Skype with his Granny.

And so when he grows and it's time to chose,
It may be Arsenal, they seldom lose.
It may be Polska, it may be Blarney,
No, he'll side with his Granda, and the Rebel Army.

Back Where We Belong

Thank you Colin Healy, we're back where we belong,
The Cross is rocking, the Shed's in full of song.
Corcoran, Coleman, Crowley & Gilchrist,
Solid as a rock, they're simply the best.
David Harrington is the club's number one,
Great with both feet, and saves goals for fun.
No shortage of talent, sitting on the bench,
Goalkeepers, strikers, and some for defence.
Chambers, McGlade, O'Connor and Umeh,
Srbely, Walker, O'Mahony and Doona.
Kargbo, Byrne, Honohan and Britton,
Crowe and Whitmarsh could easily fit in.
Bolger is strong, Healy's sublime,
Bargary and Coffee hugging the line.
Then up front we have Murphy and Keating,
When these lads are on it, it results in a beating.
We're the biggest and best supported club,
Sometimes the excess end up in the pub.
The Corner Flag, takes up the slack,
They've a private box, out the back.
We wouldn't survive without volunteers,
Too many to mention, we'd be here for years.
There's the board of management, a crew of six,
When our club was broken, they came up with a fix.
Chairman Declan Carey, always on the job,
And all for free, never asked for a bob.
The same goes for Gar, Conor and John,
Colm and Dave, they just get it done.
Special mention to those behind the scenes,
Who mind the young boys, and coach their teams.
Kearney, Murphy, McNulty & Murray,
Slow and purpose like, never in a hurry.
Thanks to our Kitman, for what you bring,
The one and only, the bould Mick Ring.
So shout it out loud, Rebels Abú,
We're from Cork and we're better than you.

Bantry Bay

The calm blue sea, turns white with rage,
Crashing into mountains, sculpting a cave.
Pods of Dolphins, rounding up fish,
Dive bombing gannets, for their favourite dish.

Humpback whales, and minkes arrive,
Shags and cormorants, preparing to dive.
It's an all-star cast, of nature at play,
In a natural theatre, called Bantry Bay.

The birds and mammals, are gone in a flash,
Galloping white horses, doomed to crash.
Winding roads, in the summer heat,
At last a rest, on Finn McCool's Seat.

Kilcrohane awaits at the base,
A pretty village, on the southern face.
A nice cold beer in Ahakista,
At Arundel's by the Sea, how could I resist ya.

What a wondrous day, as I lay in my bed,
As the sun goes down, on the rugged Sheep's Head.

Barrack Street

Walking home to where I belong,
Whistling out my favourite song.
To sing out loud, would fill me with dread,
I sound like Bowie, in my own head.
Pop into Centra for a 99,
My favourite treat in summertime.
I'm walking up the Grand Parade,
By the River Lee, where we sported and played.

I sit on the boardwalk, with others on their break,
To finish my ice-cream, and the chocolate flake.
Over Nano's bridge, I see Finbarr's spire,
To face Barracka hill, every time it gets higher.
I pass the Enterprise, and Mouse Cafe,
I'm halfway up, well on my way.
I see Elizabeth Fort and Barrack Street Band,
Keith cutting hair, scissors in hand.

Alchemy is always worth a look,
With every coffee you can read a book.
Tom Barry's Bar, they'll always greet ya,
Have a drink in the Courtyard, and Italian pizza.
If you feel unwell or your throat is sore,
Drop into Brodericks, Barry has the cure.
I round the corner, I'm on Green Street,
I'm on the last lap, I'm out on my feet.

I pass Greenmount School, the College on the hill,
Where girls and boys are learning there still.
I arrive at Roselawn, and in my front door,
Safe and sound but my feet are sore.
I've done that walk, a thousand times,
To my favourite tunes and my favourite rhymes.
A cup of Barry's, with custard creams,
Life's not too bad, as it sometimes seems.

Benno

Benno the legend, is calling it a day,
The shed will sing his name, to send him on his way.
Could play in midfield, but a defender supreme,
The heartbeat of Cork City, one of the best we've ever seen.
A towering defender, as tough as teak,
And proved it on the pitch, week after week.

Although big and strong, he played with his head,
He could play ball, left opponents for dead.
A leader of men, he led from the front,
You wouldn't cross Benno, for fear of a funt.
He won two titles, and also two cups,
And coaches the youngsters, the Rebel Army pups.

He has two caps for Ireland, and played across the pond,
With Brentford, Reading, and AFC Dons.
He played for Wycombe and Cheltenham Town,
And played with a smile, and never wore a frown.
He came back to City in 2015,
He won another title, and a cup for his team.

He's Cork through and through, with rebel blood in his veins,
The fans were always happy, with Benno at the reins.
Aside from the football, the man is a gent,
And to prove my point, he's donating every cent.
The Samaritans of Cork will benefit from his time,
And the Cork City Academy thanks to Benno, will be fine.

Some ex-City legends, we'll be lucky to see,
And underage prospects, from Cork City FC.
The Cross will be full, there's no doubt in my mind,
For Benno the legend, you were one of a kind.

Carly

My darling Carol, sweet sixteen,
The most beautiful creature, I'd ever seen.
Small, petite, with long blonde hair,
All I could do, was stop and stare.
A zest for life, always smiling,
Non-judgmental, and so beguiling.
Gypsy skirt, and frilly top,
Dancing in the Stardust, we didn't want to stop.

We'd walk out the Lough, and UCC,
Happy out, just you and me.
We'd talk for hours, about family and friends,
Saturday Night Fever, and the latest trends.
We'd go to the Capital, queue in the breeze,
At last at the window, two Jumbos please.
I'd meet you at the Farmhouse, to walk you home,
You always had a treat for me, like a cake or a scone.

So many memories, I could write a book.
The best wife, mother, and Granny,
Lots of friends, and loved by so many.
I don't dream of riches, or castles made of sand,
I'm King of the world, when I hold your hand.
Sometimes I pinch myself, to think that your mine,
The view is wonderful, up here on cloud nine.

I love you my wife, you're the love of my life,
I will love you every day, for the rest of my life.
If I was granted a wish, to end all my fears,
I wish we could have, another forty years.

Chasing Time

Heavy heart, I cannot hide,
Pulling like a dog, against the tide.
Every road, becomes a hill,
Sun is setting, I'm walking still.

I dream I'm falling, the clouds look cute,
I reach for my cord, but there's no chute.
Small stones are heavy boulders,
The sky is heavy, upon my shoulders.

My days are long, they're filled with pain,
I pray for sunshine, all I get is rain.
I'm passing through, chasing time,
With head in my hands, I'm always crying.

When they ask 'Are you OK?'
I say yes, so they'll go away.
Why can't I be. like the rest,
Always smiling, at my best.

For here I am, alone in bed,
With covers pulled above my head.
I hope one day, I can recover,
For now I'll remain, beneath this cover.

Clever Boy Shay

Shay's a counter, he counts to ten,
First in English, and Polish then.
Shay's a singer, he's the singing type,
He sings about buses, with his Granny on Skype.

Shay's a swimmer, and a good one at that,
He learned to swim, with his mommy in the bath.
He can swim, he can jump, he even does dives,
On his Daddy's back after only two tries.
He loves playing Gola he loves to score,
He'll definitely go further, of that I am sure.

When he comes on Skype, and one of us is missing,
He calls out our name to come on and listen.
His little face lights up, when he comes to the screen,
His Granny and Granda at last can be seen.
The singing and counting, can now begin,
It all looks good, for our daily Skype in.

He's only been here, for a short little spell,
But he's learned so much, that's easy to tell.
He solves puzzles with letters, and numbers too,
He can do all this, and he's still only two.

Colin Healy Pure Daycent

The chant from the Shed is, 'We're gonna win the league',
Thanks to Colin Healy, a man of intrigue.
He's a quiet man, who doesn't say much,
A tough tackling player, with a sublime first touch.

A Ballincollig man, a hotbed of sport,
Like millions before him, another export.
He played for Celtic, he won a league medal,
Then Sunderland and Barnsley, to test his mettle.

He played for Ireland, with pride and passion,
A fantastic clubman, not a follower of fashion.
He won four Cups, with Cork City FC,
A prolific winner, this side of the Irish Sea.

He's the boss at Cork City, he's giving it large,
The team are on fire, we're on a great charge.
We're playing good football, we're banging in the goals,
The league has taken notice, except a few trolls.

He's the man of the moment, a rising star,
Everywhere we go, we know who we are.
The fans are back, they never went really,
But the numbers are up, thanks to Colin Healy.

Will it end in tears, will it end in joy?
One things for certain, you're pure daycent, boy.

Cork After All

Life is full of ups and downs,
My team's been relegated, send in the clowns.
Somebody please, give me a name,
Someone to vilify, someone to blame.
As in life, It's no one's fault,
What we thought was granite, were pillars of salt.
Like all supporters, we sang we're the best,
With Tina on the tannoy, better than all the rest.
On Friday nights, we went to bed,
Reliving goals, and songs from the shed.
On cloud nine, or depressed when we lose,
Drowning our sorrows on Aldi cheap booze.

In 2017, we were living the dream,
Partying in Soho, with our favourite team.
We had glory days when we won the double,
Just a memory now my club is in trouble.
I've analysed it till my head is sore,
Listening to interviews with Trevor on The Score.
Where it went wrong, is hard to say,
Truth be told, it's on the field of play.
Right now It's black, I wont tell a lie,
When the news came through, I had a little cry.
I'll support my team, I know they tried,
Sure at the end of the day, no one died.

We'll soon be back, living the dream,
We win together, and we lose as a team.
This is not new, we've been here before,
Since the early days of 1984.
To our young fans right now, it looks black,
But have no fear, we will bounce back.
From Knocknaheeny to Togher, From Mahon to Blarney,
We'll be marching together, with the Rebel Army.
If we stick together, and sing the same song,
We'll be back on top, where we belong.
There's no quick fix, there's no magic wand,

It's City till I die, above and beyond.
Billy Murphy said it best, on the bus down to Youghal,
No one can touch us boy, we're from Cork after all.

Coronavirus Part 1

Mankind is at war, with an invisible foe,
Doctors in white suits, from head to toe.
It started in China, with a single bat,
Where it passed to a human, and that was that.
It's called the coronavirus or Covid-19,
The most deadly virus, the world has seen.
It's spreading like the plague or the Spanish Flu,
Where it all ends, we haven't got a clue.

It jumped from China, to Korea and Japan,
Europe, America, and even Iran.
It's spreading through Italy, like potato blight,
We know from our history, not a pretty sight.
It arrived in Ireland, slowly at first,
Our experts warning us, to expect the worse.
Our government's advice, is to wash our hands,
It's our biggest threat since the Black and Tans.
Wash your hands in soapy water,
The coronavirus is the Devil's Daughter.
The young and healthy, have little to fear,
It's the sick and elderly, who'll need the most care.

People on the move, the world's a smaller place,
So the virus can travel at a much faster pace.
The world is in crises, we can all play a part,
Calm heads and steady hands, will be a good start.
In times of crises, we see our best and our worse,
Where panic buying, is really a curse.
Clearing the shelves, with trolley loads of bread,
Sure if we don't have toast, we'll all drop dead.
Health is your wealth, that would always top the poll,
Now your status is zero, without toilet roll.

Coronavirus Part 2

Schools are closed, and sport postponed,
A sign the situation, is finally being owned.
We need our leaders, to be strong and wise,
Be straight with people, don't be peddling lies.
Hear this Mr President, no time for telling jokes,
Don't be telling people, it's all a big hoax.
No colour, no race, one world of skin and bones,
This is about people, not the Dow Jones.
Families are hurting, their loved ones are dying,
Gone before their time, their grandkids are crying.

We watch the news it's the same every day,
How many caught the virus, how many passed away.
Stay at home, if you go out, they're insisting,
Don't shake hands, practice social distancing.
It's surreal outside, like being ruled by a tyrant,
Heads are down, school yards are silent.
The saddest story I've ever seen,
Grandparents and grandkids, with a fence in-between.

Country after country, are closing their borders,
It's like every few minutes, we receive new orders.
You wake in the morning, and it hits you like a train,
The sorrow and sadness, of yesterday's pain.
Are we doomed to a fate of forever pining?
Does this huge black cloud, have a silver lining?
We are human beings; all we need is love,
There is no one beneath us, and no one above.
Be kind to yourself, be kind to others,
We're in this together, like sisters and brothers.

Covid Heroes

Crying in the night, can anyone hear me,
Shivering with fright, can anyone feel me.
My lungs are so tight, can anyone relieve me.
My heart is racing, can anyone save me.

A big fat fist, is squeezing my lung,
Dreaming of sessions, and songs that I've sung.
My head is pounding, every breath makes me wheeze,
I can't taste my food, I can't smell the Febreze.

I need Oxygen, I can't take a breath,
My bed's like a pool, I'm swimming in sweat.
Every muscle is aching, I can't move my hand,
I'm feeling so weak, I'm unable to stand.

Front line workers, all doing their best,
Working through the night, hardly stopping for a rest.
Less of a job, more like a vocation,
A force that's stronger, than a mighty ocean.

I start to feel better, I don't cough anymore,
I can taste my food, my throat is not sore.
Farewell front line workers, I just want to say,
You're forever my heroes, not just for one day.

Crass Putin

You bombed my house, razed to the ground,
Wailing sirens, I hate that sound.
Your missiles destroyed our houses and flats,
So now we live, underground with the rats.

You bombed our children, out of their school,
Vladimir Putin you're a terrorist, you're a fool.
Your planes are like vultures, seeking out the weak,
Stalking fleeing pensioners, who are weak on their feet.

Women and children, are put on a train,
Daddy on the platform, his face racked in pain.
They hope to make it safely to the west,
While their soldiers face the Russians, they're the best of the best.

You can hide in your bunker, ignore all the jeers,
But someday you'll be judged, in The Hague by your peers.
What sentence is fitting, no one can tell,
For you crass Putin, may you rot in Hell.

The Ukrainian people, will make you see,
There'll be no surrender, no bending the knee.
We've had evil leaders, they rise and they fall,
But you crass Putin, the most evil of them all.

The noose is tightening, I hope you feel the pain,
Crass Putin the loser, Slava Ukraine.

Cupid's Arrow

The taste of love, can be bittersweet,
Like Halloween, a trick or treat.
More often than not, it tastes so sweet,
When hands caress, and young hearts meet.

When Cupids arrow, strikes a blow,
Feelings of love, like a river will flow.
With someone you know, Or a complete stranger,
But one things for sure, it's a life changer.

Up the aisle on Daddy's hand,
Here comes the bride, strikes up the band.
Singing and dancing, with family and friends,
On the dance floor, to the very end.

Off on honeymoon, to have some fun,
Relax by the pool, in the hot summer sun.
Back to reality, now husband and wife,
Set plans in motion, for the rest of their life.

Planning for children, right now is a maybe,
It's a huge decision, to have a new baby.
For the first few years, enjoy each other,
There's plenty of time, to add another.

Live life to the full, be good to your mate,
Good things always come, to those who wait.

Darragh

Darragh has arrived, that's grandchild number six.
He has a look of both his parents, a nice little mix.
A bunter of a child, weighing nine pounds and seven.
An extra Stork was needed, to bring him down from heaven.

On his mother's side there's red men, where Liverpool are the team.
This is our year for the title, another wishful dream.
We know Darragh is clever, his team will be CCFC,
So it's off to the Cross, with his daddy, Faye, and me.

Your timing was perfect, your mammy's pride and joy,
Daddy's wish has come true, he has a big strong boy.
Our family group is growing, we were three, now we're four,
So welcome Baby Darragh, we couldn't ask for more.

We wish for things in life, like money cars and bling,
But Darragh you are priceless, we couldn't wish for one more thing.
Our house is full of laughter, there's happiness everywhere.
In every little smile, in every little tear.

We'll help you grow and prosper, mammy and daddy will show the way,
As will your friend and sister, the one and only, beautiful Faye.
When God set out on his project, the angels played their part.
Between them up in heaven, they produced a work of art.

We're feeling blessed since you arrived, and filled our house with love.
We love our handsome baby boy, thank you angels and the man above.

Declan Carey

He's a friend of mine, I treasure him dearly,
The Chairman of FORAS, one Declan Carey.
He loves the Notorious of the UFC,
And his brother Trevor up in UCC.

His dad liked a sing song, he played the box,
The heart & soul of the party, he gave it socks.
His mother ruled the roost, she was so dedicated,
Her goal in life, to see her family educated.

He's a champion web-master, for Cork City FC,
Has the trophies to prove it, if you want to see.
He won the Spiders, he was the star of the show,
Not once, but twice, that's two in a row.

I met Declan, when I sent him some pictures,
Taken at Turners Cross, at League of Ireland fixtures.
Never a bad word, if I sent a hundred or a few,
Decent to a fault, and always a thank you.

I wrote a poem, for our boss JC,
Declan did a background, had it down to a tee.
I couldn't believe, when I saw it first time,
It was such an improvement, I couldn't believe it was mine.

He's so good, like a surgeon with a knife,
I wrote the poems, but Dec brought them to life.
About two years ago, Declan had a look,
Did you ever think, of putting your poems in a book.

I never did, but if you think I could,
If we put our heads together, then maybe we should.
I wrote the poems, and just sent them in,
Declan did the editing, and did it with a grin.

He's a pair of safe hands, like Packie Bonner,
And ably assisted by Shane O'Connor.

He designed the Book, from cover to back,
And lined up the poems, in a perfect stack.

He's the Chairman of our club, and works full-time,
He worked night & day, to get this over the line.
I could never thank him, for what he's done for me,
In my wildest dreams, did I ever think I'd see.

A book by me, called Rebel Rhymes,
It's good to be alive, these are the good times.
So thankyou Declan, what I say now is true,
You've made my day bud, my dreams have come true.

Dermot Usher's Rebel Army

Usher Usher on the wall.
Came to City to play some ball.
He bought Cork City for one whole euro.
T'would cost you more, for a single Rolo.

Promising funds, to make us compete.
At the top of the league, with the football elite.
He pitched to FORAS, he spoke with pride.
He needn't have worried, it was a landslide.

He promised on match nights, the toilets would be clean,
And extra funds, to improve the team.
He doesn't want flares, because of the fines,
He even promised me, there'll be 99s.

We've struggled for years, as a fan owned club.
Five hundred souls, every month paying a sub.
Don't get me wrong, we had good times.
But it all got too much, paying wages and fines.

We wouldn't have survived, without volunteers,
Who kept our club going, down through the years.
I can hear the fat lady, sing her final chorus.
A new dawn for Cork City, not being run by FORAS.

A new era begins, under Dermot Usher.
Use a slow hand Dermot, never rush her.
We've done the right thing, we've made the right choice.
We're the Rebel Army, we sing with one voice.

There's nowhere quite like, Friday nights at the cross.
We'll sing it out loud, Dermot Usher's our boss.
We're proud Corkonians, we play to win.
We do exactly what it says on the tin.

We're not arrogant, like some will say.
We just like to win, at the end of the day,

So when we sing it, we sing it cause it's true.
We're from Cork and we're better than you.

Let's pack out the Cross, let's all go barmy.
Stand up for the City, Dermot Usher's Rebel Army.

Dylan

Granny have you heard, we have another boy,
He arrived today to add to our joy.
The labour was hard, he was slow to be born,
But worth it all, he's so beautifully formed.

The joy and happiness that Dylan will bring,
Is overwhelming for such a tiny little thing.
He's got his mother's eyes, the strength he got from Gary,
He got the best of genes, he'll be as happy as Larry.

He was born in Cork, he lives in the Déise,
Whoever he choses, we'll always praise ya.
So here's to the future, when it's time to chose,
Between his native Cork, or the Déise Blues.

If you think it's Blues, well that's just Barmy,
He'll side with his Dad, and the Rebel Army.

Emily

A date in our lives, we'll always remember,
Our Emily was born, on the seventh of November.
Our clan is growing, that's Grandchild number seven,
A most beautiful girl, sent to us from heaven.

The world is full of beautiful things,
Like the birth of a child, and the joy it brings.
Her big brother Darragh, and big sister Faye,
Will help her and guide her, and show her the way.

Her mother Sarah, is loving and kind,
You can search the world, a better mother you won't find.
Her daddy Chris, a soldier by trade,
A degree from CIT, a man that's self-made.

A three-year sacrifice, he paid for his family,
For Sarah and Darragh, for Faye and Emily.
Emily was born, in a very strange year,
A pandemic is raging, we're living in fear.

Then one magic moment, the world was serene,
When Emily was born at nine fifteen.
In trying times, we're feeling distressed,
Now thanks to Emily, we're all feeling blessed.

From darkness to light, there's a bright new morn,
For there's no better feeling, when a child is born.

Flower Lodge Where We Sported And Played

Before the days of Podge and Rodge,
We got our kicks in Flower Lodge.
Over the stiles, get in with a man,
Can you take me in Sir, of course I can.
Local heroes, and the English game,
Unknown in their homeland, here they found fame.

Big Joe in goal, great saves he would make,
Noel O'Mahony and Fada, no prisoners would they take.
John Herrick was hard, Bacuzzi had style,
Sonny Sweeney could tackle, John Lawson had guile.
John Brohan a local, Dinny Allen a Gael,
Crowds in their thousands, come rain or hail.

Donie Wallace was nippy, he played on the wing,
With Miah inside him, they made the crowd sing.
Carl Humphries, Jerry Finnegan, two boys from Leeside,
They played without fear, they filled us with pride.
The Dav was the star, he'd take you to hell,
And later that night, take your wife as well.

Frank Connelly was good, Tony Marsden was great,
Deccie O'Mahony filled in, when big Joe was bate.
Last but not least was the best of them all,
The crowd went wild, when Wiggy had the ball.
He was quick as lightning, he ran for fun,
The brightest of stars, with the power of the Sun.

Celtic on the south side, Hibs on the north side
Halcyon days, for Soccer on Leeside.
Kids in School and men down the pub,
Would debate for hours, who had the best Club.
Twenty thousand or more, on Derby day,
To watch their heroes, enter the fray.

One side depressed, on Sunday nights,
The other side elated, with the bragging rights.

My heart was broken in seventy-five,
We failed to keep Cork Hibs alive.
Woke up one morning the club was no more,
Resigned to books of Soccer folklore.

While I'm alive they'll never be dead,
With beautiful memories, I keep in my head.
When one dream dies, it opens a new door,
Cork City were born in nineteen eighty-four.
It took me awhile, I'll tell you no lie,
I'm dreaming once more, I'm City till I die.

We were Hibs, we were Celtic, Flower Lodge, Turners Cross.
We both were grieving, when our clubs were lost.
We're together now, new heroes being made,
In the City by the Lee, where we sported and played.

FORAS Or Bust

Our club is in trouble, I say with regret,
We're threading water, we're smothered in debt.
It's nothing new, we've been here before,
It's a daily struggle, the wolves at the door.
We've had numerous clubs, that couldn't be saved,
In the rebel county, where we sported and played.
But this club is different, real fans at its core,
Playing league of Ireland, since nineteen eighty-four.

Our club was almost gone, in two thousand and nine,
FORAS saved the club, and up to now, was doing fine.
But times have changed, running costs have soared,
It's all too much, for our wonderful board.
Cutting corners, to save a few pence,
It's time to face facts, no more pretence.
We can head for the cliff, like deluded lemmings,
Or consider an offer, from MR Hemmings.

Now Mr Hemmings, has a grá for Leeside,
Has the money and the will, to turn the tide.
He wants to buy the club, to save us from doom,
But first we must fix, the Elephant in the room.
The elephant in the room, is us the fans,
Is it time to admit, it's in the wrong hands.
We were lucky last year, we avoided the drop,
Not good enough for us, we should be at the top.

It's hard to compete, hands tied behind your back,
It's hard to sign players, even harder to sign back.
We can stay as we are, with a very clear vision,
Play it safe and compete in the first division.
If that's what we chose, then things will go flat,
That's not for us, we're better than that.

Our BOM reached out, to businesses in Cork,
Would you like to invest, as we're down on our luck,
But just as before, the answer was the same,

Thanks but no thanks, we've no interest in your game.
So the time has come, for the fans to decide,
What type of club, do we want on Leeside.
Do we carry on, and struggle each year,
To balance the books, and to pay each player.
Or do we let someone come in and invest,
For us to have a chance, and compete with the rest.

It's hard to change, for this was our dream,
To be fans owned, to run our own team.
We did our best, and some even better,
Playing by the rules, down to the letter.
This year was the worse, it was one big drag,
The BOM performed a miracle, pulled it out of the bag.
We could lose our club, that's our big fear,
We might not be so lucky, this time next year.
So vote with your heart, but mostly with your head,
Do we stay fans owned, or investment led.

Fully Vaccinated

Fully vaccinated, and raring to go,
Can't wait to have a meal, or maybe a show.
Meeting up with friends, and shake someone's hand,
Drop into Cypress Avenue to see a live band.
Call to my family, take the smallies to the park,
Check in when they're sleeping, that night when it's dark.
Do a shop in Penny's, for jocks and socks,
Take some photos of Shandon, and its four lying clocks.
Take a walk in Blackrock, from the river to the sea,
Then back to the Castle, for a cup of Barry's tea.

Calling to our grandkids, and a million hugs,
We've had our jabs, no more fear of catching bugs.
Down to West Cork for beaches and views,
Have lunch in Bantry, no more stupid queues.
To Youghal by the sea, along the boardwalk,
Ballycotton Lighthouse is the topic of our talk.
Ireland is beautiful, when the sun decides to shine,
Is there anything more Irish than a big ninety-nine.
Number one on my list, is a match at the Cross,
To support our players, and Colin our boss.

Nothing can beat, the Turners Cross scenes,
Cheering for Cork City, against all other teams.
It's been a hard lock down, there was day's when we cried,
For friends and family, who caught Covid and died.
No vaccine nationalism, just stop with the greed,
The rich countries of the world have more than they need.
It doesn't matter, if you're a King or a Waif,
Until everyone has the jab, none of us are safe.
Is it really over, is this the end of our pain,
Ask me again, when you see me in Spain.

Galway

We went to Galway, our very first time,
The forecast was for rain and the sun won't shine.
But typical Ireland, the forecast was wrong,
Galway bay was lovely, just like the song.
Majestic mountains and beaches so white,
That changed each day, depending on the light.
We stopped in Oughterard, for a bite to eat,
We had Cinnamon rolls, oh my God what a treat.

We saw Ashleigh falls and Killary Fjord,
So much to take in, you'll never get bored.
Kylemore Abbey, such a beautiful place,
A sense of wonderment on everyone's face.
Ballynahinch Castle, took my breath away,
Mesmerized by the tulips as the wind made them sway.
It's a paradise for walkers, a short stroll, or all day,
On the greenways you'll find, on the Connemara way.

Had a coffee in Clifden, well known for its fog,
Where Allcock and Browne crash landed in a bog.
Took a stroll on the prom along Salthill,
Climbed the diving board, oh what a thrill.
Stopped in Barna, had a beautiful meal,
For the quality of the food the price was a steal.
I saw a Busker, he was good on the fiddle,
But my one regret, I never saw Spidel.

All good things must come to an end,
Thank you Brendan for being a good friend.
Thank you Martina for your patience and time,
For my Cinnamon roll and my virtual ninety-nine.
For the whole weekend, not a care or a worry,
But the highlight for me was your delicious curry.

Gary and Trish

Gary & Trish are finally tying the knot,
Trish spun a web, and Gary got caught.
Well that's not true, I have to confess,
You see Gary bent the knee, and Trisha said yes.
Gary won the lotto, when he met Trish,
Intelligent and kind, and no mean dish.
The same goes for Trish, she hit the jackpot with Gary,
He has a heart of gold, and they're as happy as Larry.

Those early years, life was so thrilling,
The result of that, was the wonderful Dylan.
The following years things moved slowly,
But the action didn't stop, and along came Joey.
Dylan was happy to finally have a brother,
They're the best of friends, they love one another.
In the early years, life was fierce,
The economy crashed, and jobs were scarce.

They went to Clashmore, to seek their bounty,
So they said goodbye to the Rebel County.
They have a wonderful home, in beautiful Clashmore,
They have mountains and forests, and a sandy shore.
If you need a heat pump, why not give it a whirl,
Give Trisha a call, she's the heat pump girl.
Gary looks after people, just like you and me,
He works at Saint Rafael's, for the HSE.

I don't want diamonds, I don't want to be special,
If I had one wish, it's to make it official.
When it's late at night, and everyone's in bed,
And all these thoughts are flying round in my head.
Why get married, things are good as they are,
A house two kids, a dog and a car.
But something is missing, the finality isn't there,
The proof of our love, my ring finger is bare.

Now a document proves nothing,
It's a feeling inside, when I look at what I have, it fills me with pride.
Like the moment you close your eyes,
Just before you fall asleep,
That feeling of serenity, what we have, we will keep.

Gearoid Morrissey

Gearoid Morrissey, a neighbour's child,
When Gearoid scores a screamer, the shed goes wild.
His Granda Tommy, came from the marsh,
Where life was tough, and sometimes harsh.
He moved to Ballyphehane and reared a big crew,
A legend in the Harp, and Noel Murphy's too.
His dad Gerard, was a boxer by trade,
And soccer with Crofton, in Ballyphehane park he played.
Gearoid stood out, a star among strangers,
The best of his age, at Ringmahon Rangers.

Gearoid is from Mahon, he was a local star,
Life seemed rosy, looking on from afar.
The scouts came calling, he'd soon be a rover,
Off to Blackburn, he made the move over.
Life was good, Gearoid had it made,
Playing football in England, and highly paid.
It's hard without family, only talking on the phone,
His head was in England, but his heart was at home.
Gearoid decided, I must head home,
I can't live my life with my family on the phone.

A tough choice, but not looking for pity,
No sooner had he landed, than he signed for Cork City.
Happy again, a renewed love for the game,
It didn't take long, the whole league knew his name.
Some seasons were good, some ending in tears,
But that would all end, in a short few years.
The club had built a team, the best we'd ever seen,
They won the double in twenty seventeen.
Like everywhere else, Mahon could be tough,
Plagued by dealers, giving local kids stuff.

The Morrissey family, were rocked to their core,
Their worse nightmare, came calling to their door.
Gearoid's older brother, his name was Tom,
Another innocent victim, in an instant he was gone.

The Morrissey house, full of love and hugs,
Inflicted with sadness, by the scourge of drugs.
He'll never get over it, but time eases pain,
He focused on his football, he got back to his game.
He had great success with the City team,
Champions of Ireland, and a Cup winning team.

Gearoid is a hero, on the banks of the Lee,
From Skibbereen in the west, to Youghal by the Sea.
He's loved in the City, in Mayfield and Gurran,
In Togher, Ballyphehane, where his dad was born.
Gearoid is now captain, he'll bring glory wait and see,
He's the heartbeat of our club, Cork City FC.

Gillian Butler Leonard

Fasten your seat belts, for Gillian's story,
A tale of addiction, with blood guts and glory.
Born and bred, on the northside of Cork City,
And just like the song, she's charming and pretty.
As a young girl, she ignored the warning bell,
Thus began her descent, into a living hell.
A proud member of the traveller nation,
She felt marginalized, and suffered discrimination.
She had a big family, altogether thirteen,
Not that uncommon in the Irish scene.

She attended school at Churchfield in the City,
It was affectionately known as Marmalade City.
She hated primary, secondary even more,
She couldn't wait, to get out the door.
Drink and drugs, and robbing from shops,
Gillian found herself, in trouble with the cops.
I lived for the day, I could tell the tale,
I've made it girls, I'm in Limerick Jail.
The girls sunbathed, the boy's played ball,
The highlight was an orange, flung over the wall.

The drinks and drugs, I could no longer hide,
I'll never forget the night I almost died.
I took a load of tablets, that clearly weren't mine,
My dad came looking, and found me on time,
I was so out of it, my situation was dire.
I hadn't noticed my legs, were badly burned from the fire,
My innocence gone, and still just a teen,
Having my stomach pumped, at sweet sixteen.
Back in Jail, I'm now 20 years old,
I got the worst news, I was ever told.

I was attending school, it was hard but I tried,
Then a priest came to visit, cause my sister had died.
I served my sentence, I had time to think,
I went straight to the off license, to buy me some drink.

Drinking and drugging, t'was a very bad year,
Day after day, I wished I wasn't here.
I rang Cork Alliance, it filled me with dread,
I just wanted someone, to help clear my head.
I met this great lady, her name was Cora,
I'll spare ya the details, I think they might bore ya.

I told Cora, my life was a mess,
So I rang Tabor Lodge, could I please be assessed.
After my treatment, I had three months with renewal,
Then a stint at sober house, to polish the jewel.
I attended AA, my confidence was low,
I found the twelve steps, you reap what you sow.
I did a few courses, so people could see,
I'm not a thicko, I'm off to UCC.
My journey to here, was hard and very long,
My first day at UCC, I felt I didn't belong.

I phoned Sheila, she said everything will be grand,
Whenever I felt down, she was there to hold my hand.
I finally did something, that was just for me,
I'm a university graduate, with a first-class degree.
I'm so happy, I can use my degree,
To help out others, who are just like me.
My life I can manage, the world I can face,
I married a hunk, and we bought our own place.
This is my story, I hope I've inspired,
On how I became, Gillian Butler Leonard.

Goddess Clíodhna

Goddess Clíodhna Patron of Cork County,
Guardian of our crops, delivering us a bounty.
She loves her people, minding us all,
From the rugged Mizen head,
To the sandy shores of Youghal.
She resides in a Palace of rocks, near Mallow,
She bathes in Gougane Barra,
where the waters are quite shallow.

She's queen of the fairies,
A shepherd to our herds,
She heals the sick,
With her three singing birds.
She glides on the waves,
Guiding ships to shore,
Round the Beara peninsula,
To the harbour at Glandore.

She helped Michael Collins,
She whispered to him, heed,
If you listen to me,
Your people will be freed.
She went to Croke Park,
And let her birds sing,
While she entered the soul,
Of the great Christy Ring.

If you feel it's all too much,
And you need a little prod,
Yes, you're Irish by birth,
But you're Cork by the grace of God.

Healy's Wonder Goal

We've seen great things, before at the Cross
Comebacks, fightback s, and honour in a loss.
But what we saw this august night,
Was so rare, you'd question your sight.

Against our big rivals, we need to save face,
We have to score, to stay in the race.
We need a hero, to show no fear,
Or it's goodbye to the title, for another year.

Well there is such a man, his name is Healy,
And what he done, was incredible really.
The ball's in the air, but what is he thinking,
If I don't make this, our challenge is sinking.

He took off, like a bird in flight,
It's impossible to score, the angle's to tight.
He's trying the impossible, the bicycle kick,
There's very few, that can do this trick.

We know it's live, but it's like slow motion,
Healy is gliding, have we drank some potion.
Can he kick it, yes he can,
I wouldn't dowtcha boy, Healy's the man.

We can't believe, what we just saw,
We've got our win, when it looked like a draw.
Every kid who's kicked a ball,
In a field in Togher, or the beach down in Youghal,
Has dreamed of scoring, a goal like this,
In our dreams, we always score,
In real life, we always miss.

We've seen the film, and the photos don't lie,
But it's so much better, in our minds eye.
On Facebook and Twitter, their sharing opinions,
And also on YouTube, the views are in millions.

This is all good, but let me be clear,
To fully absorb it, you had to be there.
Was this a one off, we just don't know,
And that my friends, is why we all go.

Here Today, Here Forever

Cork City's not owned by FORAS anymore,
Sold for a euro to Mr Hemmings and Grovemoor.
We have no worries, we have no more cares,
One day we were paupers, the next billionaires.
FORAS was formed to save our club,
Five hundred souls paying a monthly sub.
All volunteers, for the love of our team,
Outstanding individuals, of the highest esteem.
We started out with just one team,
Now we have eight, fulfilling our dream.
The early years, we plodded along,
Then in twenty seventeen, we were really on song.
We won every game, with hardly a loss,
The money rolled in, as we filled out the Cross.
We won the double, two cups and a league,
All this success, had planted a seed.
We bought more players, our wages soared,
When success didn't come, the club was floored.
The team wasn't winning, the fans stayed at home,
The revenue dried up, we were skint to the bone.
The taxman came calling, the license man said no,
We were two days away, from our club being no more.
We had two sell on clauses, with Preston North End,
Who turned out to be a really good friend.
They bought out the sell-ons, paid off our debts,
Without any clauses, with no regrets.
They paid a nice fee, for us to play ball,
If we decided to sell up, we'd give them a call.
We held a meeting, with most voting yes,
It was hard to let go, it was all for the best.
It's the start of an era, a worrying time,
From listening to Mr Hemmings, I think we'll be fine.
With Hemmings at the wheel, FORAS can box clever,
We'll live up to our motto, here today, here forever.

Heroes

To our brave HSE, you are heroes one and all,
Standing shoulder to shoulder, you answered Ireland's call.
We're at war with a virus, like the world has never seen,
Wreaking havoc in its path, called Covid 19.
It's a war, like no other, no foe to attack,
Just doctors and nurses, wearing gloves and a mask.
They work all hours, they're on the front line,
Risking their lives, time after time.

The virus has no preference, for the young or the old,
Wears a crown of thorns, disguised as a cold.
The country's on lock down, no work and no school,
Social distancing, from each other, the new order, the new cool.
The truth of the matter, I won't tell a lie,
Some will recover, but others will die.
Our government made a decision, private hospital's nationalised
Desperate times bring desperate measures, so that's no surprise.

Whoever made the decision, I salute you, take a bow,
We're all in this together, we're all socialists now.
When our nation's in trouble, it brings out the best in us,
Let's support our health workers, for they are the best of us.
Their working conditions, to be frank, are appalling,
We are blessed to have them, it must be a calling.
We can all do our bit, so I'm asking you please,
Wash your hands all the time, and use your elbow to sneeze.

It will come to an end, how long, who can say,
Let's support our health workers, at 8pm every day.
It's the simple things, in what we do and say,
We can all be heroes, just for one day.

It's Princess Time

Have you ever stared at the deep blue sea,
And majestic mountains, how they came to be.
Mountains so green and waters so blue,
There must be a God, it has to be true.

I've had a moment just like this,
It's all because of this little Miss.
This little Miss, was born today,
And from here on in, she'll be known as Faye.

Did God have a hand, I just don't know,
She's a natural wonder from head to toe.
There's one thing certain, about this little Miss,
She was made from love, from Sarah and Chris.

The anxious wait went on for a while,
How are you Sarah, sure I'm fine, then a smile.
The phone call came, and I heard it's a girl,
Right then all around me started to swirl.
I said to myself this must be a ploy,
We were all certain, it would be a boy.

She'll be doted on, like only Helen can,
She'll want for nothing from her Granda Dan.
She'll be showered with love from her granny Carol,
And clothes from Penny's, will be bought by the barrel.
Granda Tone and Faye, will be checking city's fixtures,
And memories kept in mind and in pictures

We'll have to go out, and buy new toys,
'Cause everything in our house, is only for boys.
I feel so happy, I'm floating on a cloud,
Thanks Chris and Sarah, you've made us proud.

Life's journey has started for Baby Faye,
We'll all be there to help her on her way.
For this she'll have, her godmother Tina,

And 'nana Mar for the odd novena.
Let the future mind itself, things will be fine,
Like granny always says it's Princess time.

Joe's At The Wheel

The fire in Douglas was a disaster for Cork,
Some folks lost their car's, and others can't work.
I feel for the traders, big and small,
The smaller ones might go to the wall.
There's a shop that's really close to me,
A supporters' shop, for Cork City FC.

Lucky for us, Joe Langford's our boss,
Who laid out a plan, so we'd have no loss.
Things looked bad, our prospects looked dire,
But Joe won't be beaten, by flood or by fire.
Joe hatched a plan, to save the day,
He called up his friends at the MFA.

No bother Joe, bring your shop to the Cross,
If nothing else, 'twill lessen the loss.
Thank you Joe Langford, you saved the day,
I'm starting a campaign, to get you more pay.
One thing about Cork, we help one another,
We're one big family, like sister and brother.

If you're buying a present, drop in for a chat,
Joe will sort you out, with a scarf or a hat.
From disaster to hope, that's how we now feel,
We're motoring again, now Joe's at the wheel.

Joey

He came into this world, with no airs or graces,
He brought joy to our hearts, he put smiles on our faces.
He looks just perfect, his skin is like silk,
The reason for this, he's on Clashmore milk.

Mammy's the best, Daddy needs a rest,
They can do no more for the boy.
Nothing's a chore, they can't do anymore,
For Joey brings nothing but joy.

Joey has a brother, who is like no other.
It's great to watch them just chillin',
I have no doubt, when Joey speaks out,
He's first words will be, I love Dylan.

John Kennedy

This man has been volunteering, thirty years for his team,
John Kennedy is his name, from the town of Skibbereen.
His club his team, is Cork City FC,
From Vice Chairman of the club, to making the tea.

He has time for everyone, no one is left out,
Family, community, is what he's about.
There's another JFK, from Boston town he came,
Our John shares his values, not just his name.

Instead of waffling on, like some down the pub,
He asked himself the question, what can I do for my club.
I've seen him packing bags, for the youngsters, in our club,
Running quizzes and raffles, down the local pub.

Sometimes at a game, tempers can be frayed,
Depending on the day, and how the team played.
So John set up a section, where families can be sure,
There's no bad language, with positivity at its core.

I once brought my Grandkids, they got sweets and banged a drum.
Spent a week on Panadol, trying to quell the pounding hum.
We all go to games, when their held at Turners Cross,
But John travels the country, where he hires a local bus.

Where he gets the energy, it's a mystery I confess,
The FEC are on the move, on the JFK Express.
Just thinking about it, I'm starting to feel faint,
Where he gets time, he must be married to a saint.

The family enclosure, and running buses,
Working for Foróige, he never fusses.
Believe it or not, he has a family of his own,
With Chris his wife, and Mahon is their home.

They have two children, Aaron and Grace,
Don't know how he managed it, he's always around this place.

You could find him out in Douglas, or at Bishopstown reception,
I've come to the conclusion, it was by immaculate conception.

All jokes aside John, what I say now is from the heart,
You are what we are, you've created your own hub,
You are Mr. Cork City, it's your city, it's your club.

Just Gone For A Run

I'm your mother, your sister, your daughter,
Another name added to this senseless slaughter.
You say you love me, when you bring me flowers,
Yet you abuse me, for hours and hours.

I work by day, I walk by night,
I can't relax, I'm gripped with fright.
I hear your footsteps, as you walk behind,
Horrible thoughts, go through my mind.

Don't wear that dress, it's way too short,
You'll have that baby, you can't abort.
I hear these men, tell me their plans,
When will they learn, it's in my own hands.

You think it's a compliment, oh you're dressed to thrill,
I'm not your plaything, I'm not yours to kill.
We live in a world of equal rights,
We're sick and tired of these petty fights.

I want to live and feel the sun,
I want to be safe, while I go for a run.
I want to play music and sports with my friends,
I want to run, to where the world ends.

I'm young at heart, I want to have fun,
If anyone asks, I'm just gone for a run.

Kubalicious

I heard the news while doing the dishes,
What's his name, it's Kubalicious.
He has big bright eyes, gets them from his Granny,
The resemblance is scary, even uncanny.

We love little Kuba from head to toe,
His beautiful smile is always on show.
He has his mother's nature, his father's strength,
He has the whole package, he was heaven sent.

He has a big brother, his name is Shay,
Who will teach him and guide him, while they're both at play.
So the years move on, it's time to decide,
Between the land of my father's, or the land I reside.

Well it's clear to me, 'cause I'm his Granda.
He told me in a secret, Soy De Irlanda.

Lido On The Lee

A city rising is a beautiful thing,
In the home of Rory, Dave Barry & Ring.
Forts on Barrack Street, battles were fought,
Cathedrals and spires, where Finbarr taught.

Red stone Shandon, where bells can be rung,
The salmon turns golden, in the midday sun.
We're turning our gaze, back to the river,
Tall buildings of glass, where reflections shimmer.

The city docks are moving down stream,
Freeing up land, a developer's dream.
New houses and schools, a big rise in population
On the South City Docks, and down by Kent Station.

The city fathers, are looking for ideas,
To improve our city, and more overnight stays.
Niall Kenny has proposed a lido on the Lee,
Where citizens can swim, or have coffee and tea.

A fantastic idea, young and old can try,
Outdoor swimming, under a clear blue sky.
We had a lido, back in the day,
Long hot summers, up the baths every day.

I urge the Council, to open their mind,
A lido for Cork, would be one of a kind.
We have great companies, here on Leeside,
With their name on the lido, would fill them with pride.

How about it Apple, for Cork is your home,
You're not short of a bob, from selling the iPhone.

Love Nature

If you love nature, you'll understand,
Why I sing with birds, why I hold your hand.
A walk in the woods, hear the blackbird song,
The rustle of leaves, as you shuffle along.

Life is good, life is cool,
They're learning to grow things, today in school.
Our kids look at us, they think we're strange,
Why the indifference, to climate change.

The world's underwater, the forests on fire,
We need a leader, to free us from the mire.
The world needs to change, and come together,
To change how we do things, now and forever.

Greta and her friends say, yeah, yeah, yeah,
Politicians answer back with, blah, blah, blah.
Walk on the beach, feel the sand between your toes,
Watch the sunset, and the sky as it glows.

Walk in rain, feel the wind on your face,
Love is the answer, for the whole human race.
It's our choice, our decision to make,
Our future depends on which road we take.

Will you go with Greta and shout, yeah, yeah, yeah,
Or the bluffers in suits, shouting blah, blah, blah.

Mar Menor

Birds singing in the Trees,
Flags flapping in the breeze.
Mar Menor comes into view,
La Manga shimmering, in a haze of blue.

Flamingos filtering shrimp so pink,
Mud baths for pain, but boy do they stink.
Surfers zipping, along with their Kites
Spraying repellent, for Mosquito bites.

Electric Scooters everywhere,
Traveling at speed, but you still can't hear.
Volleyballers on the sand,
A mighty jump, then a smash with the hand.

Barefoot ballers, it's in their soul,
An overhead kick, what a goal.
Loud cheers, for those that are winning,
Oblivious to it all, those that are swimming.

Early evening, chatter fills the air,
People out strolling, in their finest gear.
A table for two, a starter to share,
Then paella, washed down with a beer.

A typical day, on the Mar Menor,
Always fun, never a bore.
On the way home, a shoulder to borrow,
Nice thoughts fill my head, we go again tomorrow.

Marley

Hello Marley Tobin, so gorgeous and so alive,
Born in CUH, at twenty-to-five.
You have Daddy's nose, and eyes like your mother's,
And a cheeky smile, just like your two brothers.

I carried you inside me, with love and care,
I prayed for this day, I can't believe that you're here.
You're a perfect baby, from your head, to your feet,
Two boys and a girl, our family is complete.

You'll be Daddy's little girl, the apple of his eye,
Our shining star, plucked straight from the sky.
Dylan will love you, a boy like no other,
And so will Joey, who's now a big brother.

We'll take you places, like Ardmore and the V,
And over the border, to Youghal by the sea.
We'll take you to Cork, to see Granny and Granda,
Bake cakes with Granny Carol, feed the fish with Granda Panda.

Your Nana Meehan, will shower you with love,
And your Granda Tomás, watching down from above.
I promise you Marley, you'll be loved forevermore,
Break out the champagne, there's a new girl in Clashmore.

Marlogue Wood

Marlogue stands proud, at the tip of Great Island,
A national treasure, for the people of Ireland.
At one with nature, while out for a scove,
A hidden gem, for the people of Cobh.

There's wonderful views, for you to find,
As you stroll among giants, of Monterey pine.
First and foremost, it's natures home,
Where birds and animals, are free to roam.

You enter the wood, to the sound of wild bees,
And rays of light, bending through trees.
There's blue tits and finches, every type of bird,
A chorus of birds' song, all vying to be heard.

There's native squirrel, scurrying overhead,
With bushy tails, and native red.
There's badgers and hedgehogs, and bats in a box,
And if you stay quiet, you might see a red fox.

There's tracks and trails, for you to explore,
There's one that leads you, right down to the shore.
There's views of Cork Harbour, and lovely wild cherry,
And stunning views, of nearby East Ferry.

There's wooden benches, to sit and drink tea,
Among scented pine, and the smell of the sea.
Go visit Marlogue Woods, release your inner child,
There's nothing more satisfying, than the call of the wild.

So, leave it as you found it, majestic and pristine,
Take your litter home, keep Marlogue Woods clean.

Match Night At The Cross

It's Friday night, I'm off to the Cross,
Hat and scarf, I say goodbye to the boss.
With Alan my brother, we go together,
Hail or shine, in all kinds of weather.

Like thousands of others, we have a routine,
Supporting Cork City, our favourite team.
Through Deerpark, and Derrynane Road,
To Turners Cross Stadium, that's our abode.

I love match night, not just for the game,
Meeting old friends, they all know my name.
Colm selling programs, setting the scene,
One of many volunteers, on the match night team.

In the ticket hut, we have Helen and Mairead,
For the good of our club, don't expect to be paid.
Through the gate, for a game of ball,
The Curragh Road stand, standing proud and tall.

Eoin and Mark, making money for the club,
As the fans stream in, from home and the pub.
I see Gerry and Rob, Tony and Dave,
Always up for a chat, or a friendly wave.

I walk to the shop, to see Dave and Joe,
Selling hats and scarves, with a big hello.
I chat with our chairman, Declan Carey,
Colin Power and Nevin, and his mother Mary.

I see the famous Moses, as sound as a pound,
His voice can be heard all over the ground.
Always remembering, Squeezer O'Donovan,
And her loyal friend, Maria O'Sullivan.

Cáit and Amy, easy to approach,
Amanda and Gina, a future coach.

I walk to my seat in the Derrynane Stand,
I see Kieran and Ken, and I shake their hand.

I meet Regina, a very big fan,
Shouting encouragement, as loud as she can.
I meet Danny Boy, always something to say,
He managed my football team back in the day.

I get to my seat, same faces all the time,
I now regard, as good friends of mine.
Jim, Mary, Paul and James, just a few of the regulars' names.

There's Finbarr, Jason, Mick and his son,
Another few names, but I'm still not done.
There's Stephen Buckley, and his daughter Ellen,
Two important people, of the story I'm telling.

We have Mark and Bernie, hoping for glory,
Their daughter Stephanie, and friend Dave Morley.
St. Anne's is the stand for other clubs,
They're only here to see City, and the late-night pubs.

The Donie Ford, is the number one stand,
With fans and dignitaries, and even a band.
John Kennedy has given our club great exposure,
Embedded in the community, through the Family Enclosure.

With Pat and Damien, there's too many to mention,
Bringing youngsters from afar, for a night full of tension.
The children kitted out, sit together in a line,
To play a five-a- side, on the pitch at half time.

Stephen Malley, blows his trumpet, it fills the City air,
The children waving flags, c'mon City is the cheer.
96FM, RedFM, RTE and Eir Sport,
Get the message to the masses, through their match night reports.

Trevor and Ken do 96FM reports,
Colm and Ruairi for RedFM Sports.

Dignitaries and sponsors, in prime position,
Tea and biscuits at half time, a City tradition.

The odd celeb might cause a scene,
Like Mick McCarthy, or our own Roy Keane.
The next section, has proper fans,
The best seats, of all the stands.

This is a name that's well deserved,
For every season they have a seat reserved.
The lower seats are out in the rain,
Fair play to Ryan, Colm and Shane.

Fair play to Aaron and Manus too,
Chris and Faye the Donie Ford crew.
Onto the Shed, the Curragh Road stand,
With singers and shouters and a one drum band.

The right-hand side, I call the Gary Mac End,
With Cian Hennessy my little friend.
Gary Mac is our number one fan,
No ifs or buts, he's the top man.

Cian's a Rebel wheeler, who Nana Bernie keeps in line,
Taking care of her grandson, and a good friend of mine.
At the other side, we have Block A,
FORAS members who are here to stay.

Two Pats, Darren and a fella called Neenan,
Dunnocks, Andrew and Damien Sreenan.
The loudest in the Cross, were the boys in the corner,
Every Friday night playing a stormer.

Opposition players, they liked to goad,
Whether playing at home or on the road.
Right in the middle, there's Commandos and Sheddies,
Waving flags and banners, with scarves at the ready.

There's one family, I like to remember,
Carmel, Eileen and Denis, a founding member.
Volunteering is in their blood, different traits they all bring,
A former Chairman, now the kit-man, Mick Ring.

There's one man missing, a stalwart, back in the day,
A legend of our club, Mr Finbarr O'Shea.
We as fans, share the same dream,
Supporting Cork City, our favourite team.

To win a league, or even a cup,
Sometimes we're down, and sometimes we're up.
No games at the Cross, we must all stay at home,
Staying in touch with each other, by Twitter on the phone.

Put aside your dreams, of football for a while,
The sound of the click, from a rusty turnstile.
Soon we'll experience, when this is over,
The smell of cut grass, and the four-leaf clover.

The cheer from a punter, I've won the bet,
At the sound of leather, rippling the net.
At the final whistle, the crowd going barmy,
As the crowd stand up, for the Rebel Army.

Just hold tough, continue to dream,
'Til we're back at the Cross supporting our team.
We'll come back in our thousands, that's not surprising,
Is there anything more beautiful, than a City rising.

Me Da Un Té

Every summer we go to Spain,
To get sun on our backs, to get out of the rain.
We like the beach, and lying by the pool,
Find a shady spot, or a comfy stool.

The different accents, and fashion would grab ya,
While drinking on the strip, and listening to Abba.
Over the years, we've seen different trends,
But this year was special cause, we made new friends.

Rory and Pauline, from Limerick town,
Always smiling and never a frown.
Pauline is funny, she talks with her hands,
Rory likes music, he likes different bands.

We drank in Riordan's, we danced in Yolo,
Will took the kids home, and Leslie went solo.
Rory was a soldier, he's now pensioned off,
Pauline delivered leaflets, to make a few bob.

So they came to Spain, for a six month stint,
When October comes around, I'd say they'll be skint.
We kept in touch by WhatsApp, and on the phone,
We swam in the Med, and met God in Mazzarón.

We ate in Quesadas, where the service was good,
Would I go back again, I certainly would.
We spent big money as a treat, in the fishbowl,
Would I go back again, I would in me hole.

The morale of this story, it's not all about the money,
It's the company you keep, and it helps if It's sunny.
We'll take home great memories from our newfound friends,
Like all good things, it's sad when it ends.

I refuse to feel sad, I refuse to feel blue,
Shur the cocktails were flowing, and we met Melissa Moo.

It's always hard to say goodbye,
And twice as hard with dirt in your eye.

I'll be counting down the days, till I hear Pauline say,
Give that lot coffee and Me Da Un Té.

Mid-life Crisis

I wish I could be, like your man on TV,
Plenty of friends, and a big salary.
Dancing in night clubs, to the latest rage,
With my latest friends, that are half my age.

Everyone loves me, I am a big star,
A house in the country, and a big fancy car.
I have people's ears, they laugh at my jokes,
The ladies love me, I'm the envy of blokes.
I say two words, they go ha ha ha,
Beginning to wonder is it all mocky-ah.

I miss my wife, and the way she would say,
See ya later love, enjoy your day.
Quick as a flash, she'd keep me on page,
Cop yourself on boy, and act your age.

But I'd look at this, as a put down and demeaning,
Memories of my youth, sure there's no harm in dreaming.
The danger is when, dreams become real,
And the layers of your life begin to peel.

So be careful what you wish for, to yourself be always true,
For it's your family and your friends, who are always there for you.

Missing Normal

I miss the sound, of heavy traffic,
Or students partying, making a racket.
Walking in groups, out the Lough,
Or kids on the street, playing run away knock.

The hoards in Penny's, searching for a bargain,
Or Woodies DIY, buying plants for the garden.
I miss the boardwalk, watching the world go by,
Or a coffee in Electric, and people saying hi.

I miss the queue waiting for a bus,
And the latest fad, being freely discussed.
I miss the football, out in the Cross,
And sport in general, it's a huge loss.

I miss the music, of Match of the Day,
It eased my mind, at the end of the day.
Oh the quietness for a while, held some intrigue,
I'm dying inside, for some Champions League.

I miss my grand-kids, asleep on my chest,
Their squeaky voices saying, Granda you're the best.
I miss collecting, the smallies from school,
Or a pint in my local, on my favourite bar stool.

I miss my family, coming round for dinner,
Being stuck inside, I haven't seen a sinner.
I shouldn't crib or have a moan,
I've a wonderful wife, and a wonderful home.

We're social animals, we like to mix,
Or a bit of devilment, or play a few tricks.
We're stuck for a while, in a movie scene,
While praying for a genius, to invent a vaccine.

Mon

Our hearts are broken, our angel is gone,
Our golden girl, simply known as Mon.
Joined at the hip, with her Mother Peggy,
Then later in life, with John her Daddy.

She went to school, at Queen of the Angel Nuns,
Then home to Reeds Square, for cream doughnut buns.
An innocent child, a cailín bán,
Well known in Douglas, through Eileen and Seán.

Everyone loved her, she was one in a million,
Brought smiles to Aghada, through Richard and Lillian.
When both parents passed, she came to depend on,
Her sister Martina, and her husband Brendan.

She lived for Saturday, the days she would count,
For a weekend with Carol and Tony, up in Greenmount.
She loved to travel, to fly away,
To Margaret and Brian, in the USA.

Anthony and Andy, so much presents, they bought her,
On her numerous trips, across the water.
London was her favourite, down the Thames from a jetty,
Big Ben and Tower Bridge, with her Dad and Betty.

Her nieces and nephews, spoiled her rotten,
She was their centre of attention, that won't be forgotten.
The jokes and slagging, she was happy as Larry,
She had a special bond, with her nephew Gary.

Your tablets and your eye drops, she would always remind ya,
Google Calendar in the Ha'penny place, when it came to our Monica.
With four or more people, Mon felt enabled,
Cheers to everyone sitting at the table.

Then out of the blue, while we're sipping our teas,
What did ye all think of my steeped peas.

She worked and lived, with Cope Foundation,
Such wonderful people, the pride of our nation.

From Hollyhill, and St. Anne's on a stool,
To St. Francis Gardens, her home in Blackpool.
The search word Queen, like a dog with a bone,
Have one look at this, I did it all on my own.

Some girls like diamonds, a fur coat would be nice,
Mon would prefer a coffee, and custard slice.
A lighthouse is a beacon, for those in bad weather,
Monica's shining light, kept us all together.

She was a simple girl, who liked simple things,
God made her special, she had angel wings.
She's at peace now, for Mon no more toiling,
Come on away up Mon, the kettle's boiling.

Mouse

As I walk up Barrack Street, heading for home,
I stop at Mouse, for a coffee and a scone,
You can sit and chat, or go online,
Or write a poem, for the washing line.

You could meet people, from Paris or Rome,
Who have moved to Cork, and now call it home.
I feel relaxed, my coffee was nice,
In fairness to Mouse, at a very good price.

I feel recharged, I needed to chill,
I think I'm ready, to face that hill.
Goodbye and thank you, to all at Mouse,
For your hospitality, on the way to my house.

If you feel like a coffee, with some news to share,
Drop into Mouse, and pull up a chair.
If your English or Irish, Corkonian or Scouse,
Come in and sit down, you're all welcome at Mouse.

My Lucky Stars

I like to sit, and stare at the sky,
By night when it's dark, and wonder why.
Why certain stars, shine so bright,
While others flicker, with dimly light.

Some like to stay, in the shadow of night,
While others stand tall, in a moon beam light.
If you look hard enough, it's like their dancing,
While others dive, and others are prancing.

I once saw him, the man in the moon,
Dance with his partner, as if to swoon.
The sky at night, can be so black,
But a NASA rocket, leaves a trail we can track.

It's hard to believe, there are people on board,
Connected to earth, through a panic chord.
We know there's a star-man, watching them,
'Cause Bowie told us, he was one of them.

My favourite stars, are the Three Sisters,
They mind our grand-kids, and our own three misters.
Blessed with good looks, and doing the books,
Telling stories by night, and wonderful cooks.

These are the thoughts, I think of most,
Brings a warm fuzzy feeling, like a Sunday roast.
At last I can sleep, so I close my eyes,
I will open them again, to see the sunrise.

I must give them, a name of their own,
Just like us, Granny and Granda Tone.
The first one is Aga, a Polish star,
It's great we can see her, cause her home is quite far.

The next one is Trisha, the Clashmore star,
Not so far, we can reach her by car.

The next one is Sarah, the Cork City Star,
We can call for a cuppa, and chocolate bar.

So at night when it's quiet, when there are no cars,
I look up to the Sisters, and I thank my lucky stars.

My Moo Moo

Sitting with my Grandkids, as we normally do,
Darragh says he loves me, and calls me his Moo Moo.
Nobody knows why, and nobody cares,
I feel so blessed, it moves me to tears.

I sit on my chair, my favourite one,
Where me and Darragh, have hours of fun.
I leave the room, to make some tea,
Darragh guards my chair, It's a sight to see.

If anyone comes along, and sits themselves there,
Darragh lets them know, that's Moo Moo's chair.
If Granny sits down, he'll let out a yelp,
It's only for Moo Moo, now go to the step.

We read and play games, we have dinosaur rumbles,
And his favourite TV, is Mr Tumbles.
He's getting tired, so I give him a bottle,
It's time for a nap, take the foot off the throttle.

He's head on my chest, cuddled into my arm,
Safe and sound, he'll come to no harm.
I think to myself, life ain't so bad,
I check out his features, he's the image of his dad.
It's the simple things, so I shared it with you.
A day in the life, of Darragh and Moo Moo.

Myles Gaffney

Myles Gaffney, balladeer and poet,
Famous on the northside, for a song that he wrote.
He's famous all over, I tell you no lie,
He was born on Redemption Road, he's Northside 'til he die.

He plays to packed houses, he's the host with the most,
Then up with the Lark, to deliver the post.
Myles wrote a song, for his wonderful mammy,
Come hold my hand son, was up for a Grammy.

Myles lost his mother, at a very young age,
It's hard when your ten, to turn a new page.
His father god bless him, had just lost his wife,
To Myles he's a hero, he gave us a good life.

He wrote a great song, about the late Liam Miller,
And also Roy Keane, be a nice stocking filler.
He sang a song, for the Champ, Joe Joyce,
A few dissenting voices, an inspired choice.

Teddy Mac got a song, 'cause he played without fear.
He won two Celtic Crosses, in both codes the same year.
Joan McDermott, her story he did tell,
How the Sisters in Bessborough, made her life hell.

What happened was wrong, no ifs buts or maybe,
And what was her crime, she was having a baby.
In the battle for his time, the family always wins,
His gorgeous wife Grace, and their handsome set of twins.

There's beautiful Kacie and her brother Jake,
A happy family, together they make.
He's a proud Republican, he supports Sinn Féin,
Proud of his roots, even though he found fame.

He learned about history, from the Tones and Christy Moore,
In Uncle Liam's Fiesta, where Myles would give a roar.

Lisdoonvarna, and the devil is dead,
A nation once again, were ingrained in his head.

Myles will sing, at a stag or a hen,
Strumming his guitar, dressed out in Ralph Lauren.
Myles is a Corkman, so proud of his roots,
A working-class boy, not a man for wearing suits.

Myles told his story on The Two Norries Pod,
He's a Norrie by birth, but he's Cork by the grace of God.

Nana Mar 80 Years Young

80 years young, on the ninth of may,
Worked hard for her family, every day.
She's the eldest of ten, she helped out at home,
While others went to school, but I never heard her moan.

Worked hard every day in UCC,
And passenger ferries, that roamed the sea.
Looked after our Dad, for fifty seven years,
He passed three years ago, she's still shedding tears.

They had a good life, filled with laughter and joys,
The results of which one girl and three boys.
She knitted Aran jumpers, for wealthy Yanks,
To feed her family, so today we say thanks.

She knits little blankets, with Ballyphehane Ladies,
They're wrapped with love, around premature babies.
A Minister of the Eucharist, and kept the place clean,
At Ballyphehane Church, on Father Murphy's team.

She'd walk Cork City, no bus or a car,
Do ya need a lift Mam, sure it's not too far.
Our mother's a giver, she was never a taker,
Goes to mass every day, to worship her maker.

There's a beautiful grotto, in Marieville square,
She puts flowers and candles there year after year.
She's loved by her grand-kids and great grand-kids too,
They call for a chat, to say I love you.

Her brothers and sisters, love her as well,
She's everyone's friend, she's sound as a bell.
When young she went bowling, with her Dad one day,
A 26-ounce bowl hit a stone and went astray.

We almost lost her, I tell you no lies,
That bowl struck her forehead, right between the eyes.

How she survived, we haven't got a clue,
It wasn't her time, I think this is true.

Today we say thanks, you are like no other,
We're all so proud, to call you our mother.
You've reached a milestone, you're our guiding star,
Happy birthday mother, the one and only Nana Mar.

One In A Million

God takes the good, before their time,
He needs their love, for the stars to shine.
His star will shine around the globe,
Guiding us home while out for a scove.

He's with us when we sing, twinkle little star,
In our rear-view mirror, while driving our car.
When City is struggling down the Cross,
We'll remember the words we heard from the boss.

City 'til I die and to the beyond,
Then watch the team rise up and respond.
He respected the youth, no need to feel pity,
He made them feel proud and respect for their City.

Collecting pensions during Covid-19,
Things we're hearing now, that went unseen.
A community volunteer for the church and school,
It never changed him, always calm always cool.

He was a family man, number one in his life,
Aaron, Grace and Chris his wife.
Nothing we can say, will ease your pain,
But the memory of John, will forever remain.
From Mahon to Knocknaheeny, his face can be seen,
And way down west, to his beloved Skibbereen.

He raised money for Marymount, while running in the rain,
For his kin, for his people, to ease their pain.
You have left this place, to grace God's dominion,
God bless John Kennedy, you were one in a million.

Our Garden

We love our garden, there's a spot where we sit,
We watch the blackbird, the robin and the tit.
They're sometimes blue, they're sometimes great,
Just be patient, sit there and wait.

We watch the butterflies, and the bumblebees,
Hop from flower to flower, and pollinate our trees.
We have apples, cherries, and juicy pears,
A joy to look at, while sitting in our chairs.

We have lovely red rhubarb, and that's just a start,
To have with custard, or baked in a tart.
We have currants and gooseberries, we turn into jam,
We have lettuce and cabbage, to go with our ham.

We wrap up in blankets, as day turns to night,
Our faces flickering, in the candlelight.
A day full of memories, tucked away in our heads,
Tomorrow's another day, it's time for our beds.

Paradise

From where I sit, I can see the sea,
Kept cool by a breeze, blowing over me.
Families sitting beneath sombreros,
Lifeguards in their towers, our unsung heroes.

Lines of deckchairs in blue and white,
A nod to the sea and sky, so bright.
Boats bobbing on gentle waves,
Beach soccer goalies making world-class saves.

At the Heladería not a seat to be had,
A mint choc ice-cream, life ain't so bad.
I have one gripe, a pet hate of mine,
For love nor money, you can't get a '99.

A small price to pay, I do realize,
After all, I am sitting in paradise.

Picking Blackaas

Out picking blackaas, oh happy days,
Childhood memories, in Nana Shea's.
Out the wella, and up the old line,
With Nana Mar, in summertime.

We all head out, with buckets in hand,
After a good rinse out, to clear out the sand.
An annual outing, on fine August morns,
The only downside, a hand full of thorns.

Our buckets overflowing, with succulent fruit,
Our arms torn asunder, to tell you the truth.
Dreaming of jam, on a freshly baked scone,
We have enough now, so we all head home.

Bread and jam, we have for our tea,
The best things in life, are truly free.
Cut the bred nice and thick,
Spoon on the jam, until we're sick.

Heartburn and cramps, I can't get to sleep,
My mother shouts up, not another peep.
I finally get to sleep, all my senses are clear,
And dreaming of doing it all, again next year.

Radiothon

Giving for living, is back on the wireless,
The Radiothon team, so willing and tireless.
The children of Cork, so innocent and pure,
Need all you can spare, to help find a cure.

There but for the grace of God go I,
So put your hand in your pocket, let's pile the money high.
I'm listening at home, in a nice warm place,
With tears of sorrow, streaming down my face.

We're all one family, in Cork by the Lee,
My neighbours' problems, is a problem for me.
Children dream, to be a singer or a dancer,
Should we tell them not to dream, just because they have cancer.

Never stop dreaming, don't give up on your dream.
So give what you can, to PJ and his team.
There are living angels, at work with Cork Arc,
Just a phone call away, by day and after dark.

Marymount Hospice is the soul of Cork City,
Guardian angels by the Lee, so charming and pretty.
There are others at work, we can't name them all,
But year after year, they answer the call.

It's not just children, it strikes at every age,
With your kind donation, they can turn a new page.
Text friends on the WhatsApp, to show that you care,
Twelve Euro a month, just for one year.
So give what you can, to the Radiothon team,
The price of a meal, so that others can dream.

Rebel With A Cause

Mick Lynch, defender of the rail
Hated by The Telegraph, The Sun and The Mail.
He went on Sky News, Kay Burley had a go,
As per usual, Mick stole the show.

He went on GMB, to Mick it was a doddle,
He told Richard Madley, stop talking twaddle.
Question Time was next, where he took some abuse,
They were here for Mick Lynch, not Fiona Bruce.

He spoke to Robert Preston, where the compliments were zero,
Then revealed to the world, that James Connelly was his hero.
A champion of the left, he fights for workers' rights,
Ensuring better pay for those working nights.

Love him or hate him, he doesn't want your pity,
And the scoop of the day, he supports Cork City.
His connection to Cork, will come as no surprise,
How he fights for his mates, to get them all a rise.

He wants a fair society, to share the nation's wealth,
To stop the elites, from stealing it by stealth.
He tries to keep the money, from greedy bankers' paws,
You could say our Mick, is a Rebel with a cause.

Reflections

She tells me when my face looks haggard,
She points to where the lines have gathered.
She helps me dress, before I go out,
Then I feel good, while out and about.

She helps me shave and brush my teeth,
And buying shoes, for both my feet.
I glance at her, as I pass by,
Removing dust, inside my eye.

Lipstick, mascara, eyeliner, I trace,
And all because, you reflect my face.
Without you my friend, I'd be surely stuck,
I won't let you down, for fear of bad luck.

Seven years, is a mighty long time,
I'll keep you in shape, with a polish and shine.
On my wall, for all to see,
For personal moments, between you and me.

Rhyme For A Rebel

The nicest fella you could ever meet,
A friendly face coming up the street.
Always a smile and a word in your ear,
And a bit of a ball hop without any fear.

He took up rhyming a few years back,
He caught the bug, he got the knack.
Telling trophy tales of Cork City,
For the whole wide world to see.

His Canon surgically attached,
To snap the action every match.
If you move even an inch,
Hincha'll get you it's a cinch.

He's loved Cork soccer all his life,
As well as the lovely Carol his wife.
He idolised The Dav I heard,
The footballer he most preferred.

Cork Hibs and City his devotion,
Ups and downs, broke, promotion.
He's got his own team now at home,
Four sons, six grandkids, him in goal.

The pinnacle has now been reached,
Without anyone being impeached.
Rebel Rhymes, we all now know it,
Tony Tobin City's poet.

Poem by Darren O'Keeffe.
Written for Tony and read during the launch of Tony's first book "Rebel Rhymes" at the Cork City Library on 19th February 2019.

Rocket Man

Young Adam King, from the town of Youghal,
Gave the nation a lift, like Ireland's call.
You see Adam appeared, as you all well know,
On a Christmas special, the Late Late Toy Show.

He won our hearts, with his happy face,
As he launched Ryan Tubridy, into outer space.
He counted down, from twelve to one,
You're clear for lift off, major Tom.

The rocket flew high, the sky filled with streamers,
NASA tweeted out, come join our team of dreamers.
Commander Hadfield, was watching the show,
He Tweeted to Adam, so that he would know.

I saw your smile and your wonderful face,
Can't wait to get together, and chat about space.
Nora Patten, she watched from afar,
All eyes were on Adam, the brightest star.

Ryan hinted, someone was in the wings,
A friend to Adam, who gave him special things.
Would it be a famous actor, or even a royal,
It was Adam's best friend, the porter John Doyle.

John told us, they were part of a tribe,
For the children of Ireland, Temple Street's pride.
Adam is normal, he sweats and he bleeds,
He's just a little boy, with additional needs.

He's a happy boy, he gave our heart strings a tug,
With his big paper heart, for a virtual hug.
We must cherish all children, for our children are us,
They're not looking for pity, just make a little fuss.

Let's have a Country of equals, a safe place for us all,
Let Adam be our inspiration, the Rocket Man from Youghal.

Saint Jack

No knighthood for Jack, the Queen said no,
No room in the realm, unlike his bro.
A world cup winner, with his brother Bob,
Getting paid to play football, they had the dream job.

He came from Ashington, Newcastle upon-Tyne,
Played with Leeds United, in their famous back line.
A one-club man, he never strayed,
A legend at Leeds United, they loved how he played.

He won the lot, titles and cups,
And loved the pubs, where he had a few sups.
He finished with Leeds, in seventy three,
The first time in his life, he found himself free.

He managed a few clubs, with varied success
His head was fried, he needed a rest.
He applied for the Ireland job, he didn't stand a chance,
No one in fact, gave his name a second glance.

Someone in the FAI, gave a grenade a lob,
A surprise announcement, big Jack got the job.
He arrived in Ireland, in nineteen-eighty-six,
He set out a plan, he said he had a fix.

Some people didn't like it, an Englishman in our team,
By the end of it all, Jack would reign supreme.
He qualified Ireland for their first World Cup,
The country went mad, we were all on the sup.

With money in the pocket, the Credit Unions were mighty,
We were all on the plane, to Italia 90.
We drew with England, after Lineker scored.
When Sheedy equalized, together we soared.

I remember it well, the country went barmy,
We were all on board, part of Jackie's Army.

The whole country, went from bust to boom,
Big Jack and his team lifted the gloom.

In the eyes of the people, Big Jack was a treasure,
His mantra to the team, was put 'em under pressure.
Big Jack would talk to anyone, any Joe soap,
The most famous of them all, was meeting the Pope.

The ninety-four World Cup, in the USA,
We qualified by playing, the same old way.
A night of hostilities, under lights after dark,
North versus South at Belfast's Windsor Park.

Billy had the crowd, in the palm of his hand,
Both sides of the island, like to have the upper hand.
The North scored first, the place went wild,
For a lot of their fans, the South was reviled.

They did everything to stop us, they went out of their way,
But McLaughlin scored a screamer, to send us on our way.
He did it again, Jack showed the way,
Our second World Cup, in the USA.

In the stadium of Giants, it's rarely seen,
New York was Irish, in a sea of Green.
Ireland were underdogs, expected to lose,
Former champions Italy, those famous blues.

We did it again, we climbed the mountain,
By a wonder goal, from the great Ray Houghton.
Jack is a legend, a hero to us all,
From Galway to Dublin and Cork to Donegal.

Jack got his passport, he's officially one of us,
Has free travel on the trains, and around town on the bus.
Jack loved to fish for salmon on the Moy,
Nothing made him happier, it filled him with joy.

Soccer in Ireland was the poor relation,
Brought front and centre, that was Jack's creation.
All good things must come to an end,
But Jack's good name will always be on trend.

English by birth, under a union Jack,
Canonized in Ireland, thank you Saint Jack.

Santiago De La Ribera

On the roof there's a cooling breeze,
Birds are singing in the trees.
The Spanish Air Force whizzing by,
White trails in a clear blue sky.

Siesta time as shadows creep,
Most of Spain is fast asleep.
A dip in the sea to cool my skin,
The Med lapping against my chin.

Back to the beach, we make our retreat,
'Neath a sombrero, to escape the heath.
Back to our house for a bite to eat,
A slice of melon, a cooling treat.

Off to bed I'm feeling beat,
It's hard to sleep in the Spanish heat.
I love those dreams, the kind that transfer ya,
To my favourite place, Santiago De La Ribera.

Shed In The Sky

Farewell Finbarr, you were a legend at the Cross,
The great Pat Dolan, once called you the boss.
You were there from the start, when no one came,
Both stars rose together, now everyone knows your name.

You climbed the stands, to retrieve the ball,
You waved to the crowd, dowtcha Finbarr was the call.
Always smiling, and loved a chat,
And known as the man, with the flat green hat.

You travelled Ireland, from Cork to Derry,
And down to Cobh on the Passage West ferry.
You loved the players, and helping the team,
Minding the dressing room, and keeping it clean.

You gave sweets and Jaffas, to the kids at the match,
Up for a baa, hoping they'd catch.
You'll be remembered for your smile, and your gentleman way,
It will never be the same again, on match day.

Sleep well Finbarr, we all bid you goodbye,
God needed a steward, for the Shed in the sky.

Sixty Years Young

Happy birthday pet, you're sixty today.
Gasps from the crowd, no feckin' way.
She can't be sixty, how can that be?
She bought a drink in Aldi, and was asked for I.D.
She's the slimming world Queen, an expert on weight.
How to lose a few pounds, for a wedding or date.

She's a mother of four, and a granny of eight.
It's a miracle of nature, to look so great.
She's a fashionista, she loves her style.
Stays in shape, walking mile after mile.
You're young at heart, and still my cutie.
And well able to shake that booty.

So enjoy your meal, and a nice glass of wine.
We're booked in for the night, tonight you're all mine.

Slava Ukraine

Will he or won't he, will Putin invade?
The decision for war, was already made.
He lied to the world, he just doesn't care.
A typical bully, the people live in fear.
Putin's a tyrant, who likes to inflict pain.
He just couldn't stand, a democratic Ukraine.

In the dead of night, the bombs rained down,
Hitting people's homes, in the centre of town.
The people of Ukraine, stood up to the bear.
Like President Zelensky, they showed no fear.
They offered Zelensky, a safe place to hide.
I need ammunition, I don't need a ride.

The man's a legend, with balls of steel.
Refusing to lie down, he won't come to heel.
The world is watching, we stand with Ukraine.
We feel your anxiety, we feel your pain.
The Russian army, is reduced to a crawl.
After six days of fighting, Kyiv didn't fall.

Ukrainians are fleeing, for fear of dying.
Are you happy Vladimir, watching babies crying?
Mothers and girlfriends, hugging boyfriends and sons.
As they head to the front line, with bullets and guns.
The Ukrainian people will fight to the death.
They will not lie down, on that you can bet.

Putin the monster hits buildings with rockets.
Him and his cronies, will be hit in their pockets.
The west has put sanctions on several Russian banks.
Impacting their ability to buy missiles and tanks.
Russia is now a pariah state.
A collapse of their economy, is now their fate.

No Eurovision songs, with Russian names.
No football or gold medals, at the Olympic games.

Vladimir Putin, your name proudly stands.
With Hitler and Lenin, with blood on your hands.
Ukraine is drowning, in a river of tears.
As you murder children, while hugging teddy bears.

A famous Cork man had a similar fight.
He proved to the world that might is not right.
His name was MacSwiney, he died in Brixton jail.
"It is not those who can inflict the most,
But those who can suffer the most, who will prevail."

Strange Times

Talking through the window, it's not as bad as it seems,
And sitting in our front rooms, bingeing on streams,
It's world war three, but not as we thought,
Our gardens are our trenches, where the war is being fought.
Two kilometres at a time, that's our daily walk,
With no interactions, not allowed to talk.

Our children come to visit, but they can't come in,
It's been a month, my resolve is wearing thin.
It started in China, a place I've never been,
From a bat to a human, called Covid nineteen.
Factories are shut, the pubs are all quiet,
The kids want to facetime, ah go on so I'll try it.

It's a world pandemic, no country escaped,
I've seen every program, what I haven't I've taped.
We go to the shops, social distancing please,
Keep two meters apart, just in case you sneeze.
We'll beat this virus, if we all stick together,
Thinking of the sick, praying they'll get better.

Our hearts are broken, for those that have died,
The oceans have swelled, with tears we have cried.
Some say don't worry, soon there'll be not a trace,
say that to our health workers, say that to their face.
To our front-line workers, I'd just like to say,
You are heroes to us all, facing danger every day.

When this all ends, just imagine the scene,
Until then we carry on, till they find a vaccine.

Sunny Days

Sunny days catching rays;
On east Cork beaches,
And west Cork Bays.
We're lucky in Cork, much more than most,
With miles and miles of wonderful coast.

Barleycove's pure white sand,
Barefoot lovers, walk hand in hand.
Driving the Beara, O'Sullivan's home,
Breathtaking views, recorded on my phone.
Sun is high, sunglasses and a hat,
Glistening waters, along the goat's path.

Garryvoe and Youghal by the sea,
Ham sandwiches, and a flask of tea.
Gathered round, we sit and talk,
Then walk it off, along the boardwalk.
Load up the car, we head for home,
Arrive in Killeagh, we stop for a cone.

It's everyone's favourite, it's yours and mine,
Ice-cream and a flake, the good old 99.

That's What Life Is All About

When I was young, and you were strong,
We always fought, 'cause I was wrong.
Then I grew up, and saw the light,
Now we are friends, and never fight.

You showed us all, how we should live,
Never take, but always give.
Positive thinking, never strife,
Be out in front, partake in life.

Life's for living, never mundane,
See the world, jump on a plane.
Look the world, right in the eye,
Laugh out loud, and sometimes cry.

Family first, then your fellow man,
Do your best, do what you can.
It's the end of an era, a huge void to fill,
A light is gone out, up in Hollyhill.

So don't be sad, don't despair,
The lessons he taught us, will always be here.
Let bygones be bygone, raise your glass to an icon,
Sip your whiskey, sip your stout,
With one voice, we will shout.
That's what life is all about.

The Big Fella

He was known as the big fella, and sometimes the boss,
He was born in Clonakilty, in a place called Sam's Cross.
A strange thing happened, when Michael was born,
His father declared on that faithful morn.
He said Michael would be lost to this place, to this town land,
But would do great things for his country, his homeland.
He lived with his sister, from Clon she did hail,
He would soon head to London, as a clerk in the Royal Mail.

Michael kept in touch, with things across the foam,
How the people were mistreated, by the tans back at home.
Michael met a man, by the name of Sam Maguire,
Inside young Collins, he helped light a fire.
The spark took hold, the fire turned to rage,
Collins headed home, to write history a new page.
He headed off across the Irish sea,
A member of the GAA, and the IRB.
He joined the fight, which wasn't surprising,
Stood fast with his comrades, in the Easter Rising.
He fought the good fight, the fighting was fierce,
Inspired by Connolly and Padraig Pearse.
The G.P.O. was in ruins, with no roof or a stamp,
The Brits sent Collins to Frongoch internment camp.

He rose through the ranks, of the volunteers,
As the head of Sin Fein, he had the politicians' ears.
A TD for South Cork, A minister of Finance,
When Collins spoke, he had the people in a trance.
In 1919 Collins would have his say,
The twenty first of January, is our independence day.
In the war of independence, he was chief of staff,
With one sole aim, get the Brits out of our Gaff.
From here on in, Collins would declare,
We'll fight fire with fire, it's guerrilla warfare.
Collins had charisma, there was nothing not to like,
He dodged the British army, riding round Dublin on his bike.
Life wasn't easy, he wasn't living for the thrill,

He got no gruesome pleasure, giving orders out to kill.

Collins had good friends, but no one very near him,
But that would all change, when he met Kitty Kiernan.
He had contacts in the Castle, he had friends from his homeland,
But his right-hand man, was his friend Harry Boland.
His Chief was De Valera, their friendship was quite fleety,
He sent Collins off to London, to negotiate a treaty.
He signed a deal, not by heart, but by head,
He knew when he signed it, he would end up dead.
We got our Republic, except for the north,
He believed it was a stepping stone, in the future he would sort.
He won our independence, we left the UK too,
And formed our republic, in 1922.
He won the war with Britain, but another had begun,
Where Brother fought with Brother, Father fought with son.
The anti-Treaty forces, were not happy with the deal,
So they took up the Gun, to show how they feel.
Collins went to Cork, to speak with his foe,
TO bring them on board, to give the Republic a go.

The IRA weren't happy, they didn't like what they saw,
A sniper's bullet finished Collins, in a place called Béal na Bláth.
The war eventually finished, two parties in the Dail,
Fine Gael for Collins, and DE Valera's Fianna Fail.
The war is a long time over, but the bickering goes on,
The people are losing patience, they better cop themselves on.
Ireland has changed in so many ways,
It's open and tolerant, unlike the bad old days.
I believe that Collins would approve if he could see,
We're upward we're mobile, no more bending the knee.
So rest easy Michael Collins, Sleep well within your grave,
You were the mightiest of men, you were the bravest of the brave.

The Blood and Bandage

Beautiful Cork on the banks of the Lee,
From Gougane Barra, to Youghal by the sea.
In Midleton Town, for a whiskey surprise,
To Ballycotton cliffs, to watch the sunrise.
The men from the east, stand proud and tall,
Cú Chulainn's army, they love the small ball.
Hurlers live here, their speed will thrill ya,
Castlemartyr, Imokilly & the boys from Killeagh.

Mallow Town, jockeys jump for joy,
A bowl of odds, to the town of Fermoy.
On to Charleville, in the summer breeze,
You can't bate the taste, of Mitchelstown cheese.
At the end of the road, on the Mizen head,
A bright red sky, as the sun goes to bed.
Ballers live here, toe to hand,
Over the bar, to cheers from the stand.
Bantry and Bandon, a hurley's rarely seen,
The same in Dunmanway, and the town of Skibereen.
Inchydoney strand, there's surfers galore,
Garnish Island, where eagles soar.
Clonakilty town, and then Sam's Cross,
Collins country, the home of the boss.
Bandon town, gateway to the west,
Turn right for Dunmanway,
Where Sam's laid to rest.

Into the city, to the heart of the marsh,
Where life can be wonderful,
And sometimes quite harsh.
Finbarr lived here, with trees and green fern,
Where Finbarr taught, let Munster learn.
The City's divided and so is the river,
To the South Gate, to the North Gate,
With your goods to deliver.

Up Shandon Street, where houses do clutter,
Towers and churches, built with money from butter.
Shandon steeple, you can see it for miles,
The sound of the bells, fills the city with smiles.
The North Cathedral, with its red sandstone,
One half of the city, call this part their home.
Down Blackpool and onto the Glen,
Where Ringy was the king, the mightiest of men.
The Men and their hounds, dragging meat for a thrill,
Downing Murphys and Beamish, to the boys of Fairhill.
Over in Mayfield, lived the greatest ever seen,
On the playing Fields of Cork, the bould Roy Keane.

Across the river to the southside of town,
JBM rules here, he wears the crown,
Big ball, small ball, and ball on the ground,
Would be seen around Greenmount with his faithful greyhound.
Gerald to Charlie, no relation at all,
Just a pair of McCarthy's who loved to play ball.
The Barrs and Nemo, the stars of GAA,
And Robert Heffernan, he could walk all day.
Briege Corkery, Rena Buckley, they played both codes,
All-Ireland medals by the barrow loads.

O'Gara, O'Mahony on the rugby field,
Sonia and Derval, endurance and speed.
From Togher Denis Irwin, Turners Cross Dinny Allen,
Jack Doyle from Cobh, on board the Innisfallen.
Fearless Decky Daly, outrageous Patsy Freyne,
John Caulfield, Pat Morley, just a few to name,
Dave Barry played soccer and also GAA,
Wouldn't dowtcha boy, you always saved the day.

Not forgetting, Morgan, Cummins and Larry,
He lofted the viaduct, the bould Mick Barry.
Cork is known as the rebel county,
Tom Barry and his men, on their heads was a bounty.
They survived in the mountains, they watched each other' back,
Won the day at Kilmichael, where they lowered the union jack.

Our county colours, are red and white,
Our opponents dread us, it fills them with fright.
Our banner will always play to our advantage,
Up the rebels, here comes the blood and bandage.

The Dermonator

Went into Cork city, to buy a new pants.
Walked by Herlihy's Centra, just by chance.
That's when I saw it, for the very first time.
This guy was pulling a huge 99.
I had to ask, are you the creator?
I am indeed, it's the Dermonator.

I was very impressed, and a little surprised,
How it all stayed together, because of its size.
I said young man, that's a work of art,
It's not about the finish, it's all about the start.
He moved quite slowly, going anticlockwise,
Building the base, to maximize the size.

From start to finish, not a drop did he spill,
It's so big and impressive, like St. Patrick's hill.
Then the flake, was positioned with skill,
I don't think I ever got such a big thrill.
When he placed it in my hand, I couldn't speak,
If I start straight away, I might finish next week.

Take my advice, if you want to cool down,
Head into Herlihy's in the centre of town.
In the middle of Cork City on Patrick's Street,
Give yourself and your family a 99 treat.

The Fairies

A Fairy came to me last night,
Her wings fluttering, and bright as a light.
She didn't scare me, I didn't get a fright,
She was shiny and sparkly, a beautiful sight.

I lost a tooth, the day before,
With a little luck I'll lose some more.
When I smile, I look real funny,
But thanks to the Fairies, I'm in the money.

The Girl from Portland Row

Our golden girl, from Portland Row,
Queen of the ring in Tokyo.
She's the pride of Dublin and Ireland too,
Won gold for Ireland, one of the chosen few.
She beat the world champion, a girl from Brazil,
Left hooks and body shots, she went for the kill.

Boxing clever, using the ring,
Back in Dublin they started to sing.
Her mother Yvonne, can't watch her fight,
She sits in the garden, well out of sight.
She relies on hubby, Christy and the boys,
She knows it's going well, when they make lots of noise.

She lost the first round, but only just,
Then all guns blazing, win or bust.
She cruised the second, and won the third,
Then the loudest cheer Ireland's ever heard.
"We're all champions," that was her quote,
Such a humble person, not one to showboat.

She stood on the podium, with tears in her eyes,
She raised the tricolour, she won the top prize.
As we say in Ireland, she gave it welly,
With millions at home, glued to the telly.
We threw every punch, we took every hit.
Roaring her on, Kellie keep her lit.

At the final bell, her hand raised high,
Her emotions burst free, now she could cry.
As she watched her flag, slowly rise,
The camera zoomed in on Kellie' eyes.
Emotions pent up, for many years,
Released in an instant, in a flood of tears.

Scenes await her, when she gets home,
At last human contact, instead of the phone.

It's been a bad year, but we're hale and hearty,
Now thanks to Kellie, it's time to party.
Kellie's our hero, she's simply the best,
Her couch is calling, she needs a long rest.

Let's give her some space, let's all take it handy,
Give her time to unwind, with her partner Mandy.
Thank you Kellie, we have reason to cheer,
I'd say I wasn't the only one, to shed a wee tear.
From here on in, till the day you grow old,
There goes Kellie Harrington, the girl that won gold.

The Godfather

To my grandson-godson-Joey,
I can't believe that you chose me,
Of all the fish in the deep blue sea.
I'll make you a promise, 'cause I want you to know,
I'll be there for you always, to help you to grow.

I'll be there on my stool,
for your first day at school.
I'll join the parent's union,
for your first Holy Communion.
I'll be the one, to buy the PlayStation,
I'll be at your side when you make your confirmation.

I'll be there in the future, with the latest trends,
You can tell me the gossip, on your latest girlfriends.
Later in life, you'll have all this knowledge,
You can take it to work, or even to college.

Then one day, right out of the blue,
Someone will say Joey, I chose you.
You can use these words, there is nothing I'd rather,
I'm so proud and honoured to be your godfather.

The Last Echo Boy

The last Echo boy working in Cork City,
If no one takes his place, 'twill be such a pity.
The sound of "Da Echo" could be heard through the air,
Another tradition gone, does anyone care?
I remember the city, filled with noise,
Get your Echo, your Examiner, shouted the Echo boys.
One by one they disappeared,
When digital media overnight appeared.

So treasure David Hogan, He's so rare yet so real,
Drop by and buy the Echo, and say how you feel.
He's an icon of our city, he's the last Echo boy,
Like Shandon's bells, his sound brings us joy.
You'll find him in town, outside the GPO,
Selling "Da Paper" to those on the go.

A pleasant chap, always up for a chat,
About local issues, and this and that.
He's out in all weather, he has no fear,
He stood up, he walked out, left behind his wheelchair.
He works very hard, for very little pay,
To visit his sister in the USA.
I admire David, I think he's great,
He deserves his break, in the lone star state.
Don't take him for granted, 'cause he's the last one,
When David retires, the Echo Boys will be gone.

The Lough

Out the Lough, we all stroll around,
The outer ring is one mile around.
The inner ring, is for sight and sound,
Where swans and ducks are splashing around.

The Hawthorn bar, a nice place for a rest,
Where the views of the Lough, are always the best.
Sit and relax, with a coffee and scone,
Or a quart, with your friends, before you head home.

O'Connell's products are always delicious,
Sausages and rashers, and turkeys at Christmas.
Lough pet supplies, you can spend a few bucks,
On a big bag of seed, to feed the ducks.

The fitness fanatics, are out there speed walking,
While others stroll in pairs, and spend their time talking.
I like to bring the smallies out the Lough for a walk,
Stop off at the swings, feed the ducks, have a talk.

I remember as a boy, in the summertime,
Fishing for rud, till well past nine.
Others would come, from a faraway land,
For specimen carp, the biggest in the land.
Then for the smallies, how could we forget,
Catching torn eels with a bamboo net.

There's the Lough Ceilí, for locals and tourists,
Where the goal is for fun, not just for the purists.
On Wednesday nights, bring your dancing shoes,
And dance the night away, in groups or in twos.

There's an ancient tradition, that's still going strong,
Where the local children, bring their hurleys along.
They march in line, with hurleys in hand,
Down the Lough Road, with the Barrack Street band.
It's jumpers for goalposts, nothing too lavish,

But there's no holding back, representing your parish.

We're lucky to have it, such a place, and for free,
An oasis in the city, so much nature to see.
The Lough is for us all, it's beauty to behold,
Whether young and fit, or slowing down 'cause you're old.
So put on your runners, and do a few rounds,
Whether walking against the clock, or to lose a few pounds.
I couldn't finish up, without this story, I suppose,
When we walked on water, one winter when it froze.
Or walking with your lover, hand in hand, on a jag,
Or supping cider, or smoking your first fag.

We all have great memories, of this wonderful place,
It never fails to bring a smile to my face.
Let's treasure and protect it, we have to make sure,
That it's here for our children, that it's here for evermore.

The One Percent

I cling with one finger, to the bottom rung,
On the ladder of life, my song is sung.
I lost my job, I lost my house,
Don't feel like a man, I feel like a mouse.
A Simon bed, a penny dinners meal,
My faith restored, like a man I feel.
Necessities of life, but heaven sent,
I wonder what it's like, for the one percent.
More money than sense, because of greed,
While families are homeless, they take no heed.
A hotel is our home, for a family of four,
All in one room, and no front door.

The elderly on trollies, looking for a cure,
No dignity or respect, because they are poor.
When they knock at the door, in their fine topcoats,
Promising the world, if you give them your votes.
Remember them well, remember their face,
When you cast your vote, put them in their place.
'Cause they just don't care, they have no shame,
There'll be no change, it's always the same.
When the country's in trouble, and there's war to be done,
The one percent has one voice, give the poor man a gun.
Here's some bullets and a pat on the back,
We're all behind ya, when you're under attack.

You'll do us proud, for we know that you can,
Follow our orders, go kill your fellow man.
I like the saying, that health is your wealth,
If you're rich, you're healthy, if you're poor, tighten your belt.
How do these men, get to rule without fear,
I've studied their form, now the answer is clear.
In my younger days, I admit, I was flummoxed,
All you need is a neck, like a jockey's bollix.
When the preacher is threatening you, with heaven or hell.
Tell him this is our country, it's for the poor man as well.

The Simple Things

I'll never take for granted, my freedom to roam,
Or licking a 99, five kilometres from home.
Watching city play football, at the Cross,
Or working from home, on zoom with the boss.
Going to the shops, is a daily task,
Not recognizing your friends, 'cause they're wearing a mask.
Posting pictures, how it started until now,
Facebook and twitter, for this, take a bow.

Walking every day, on the same bloody street,
It's painful and boring, like the blisters on my feet.
Ireland is beautiful, except for the rain,
How I long for a week, on a beach in Spain.
Here we have lock downs, and people on furloughs,
Instead of waking to sunshine, with chocolate and churros.
Meeting our loved ones, through a window frame,
Not holding them tight, just isn't the same.

Bingeing on movies, and TV shows,
Taking pictures of starlings, blue tits and crows.
Who'd have thought, that Pennys is a treat,
Buying underwear and T-shirts, and socks for your feet.
Football and sport, is rubbish without fans,
Drinking too much wine, and way too many cans.
It's the simple things, we should treasure in life,
Like your parents, your children, your husband, or your wife.

We'll get our old lives back, they're rolling out the vaccine,
Meeting up with our friends, watching our favourite team.
We've all learned a lesson, from our lives being shattered,
It was always the simple things, in life that mattered.

Timmy's Story

My name is Timmy, I won't keep ya long,
I'll tell you my story, like a poem or a song.
I remember as a boy, being hungry all the time,
And the man of the house, at the age of nine.
I had two brothers, and my mother at home,
No father to guide us, we were left on our own.
My mother did her best, it was hard to get by,
She had problems of her own, but by God did she try.

I felt useless in school, it was boring like mass,
I spent most of my time, at the back of the class.
I was bullied on the street, he filled me with fear,
One day I fought back, I had found my stare.
I faced the bully down, his fear I could detect,
He never bothered me again, I had gained his respect.
In a nearby shop, we robbed to get by,
Tippex and Varnish, that we sniffed to get high.

We dabbled with Es and sometimes hash,
We robbed houses and cars, and bought drugs with the cash.
I was selling drugs, I thought I was crabbit,
I was making money, just to feed my own habit.
My wife and two kids, at home on their own,
Big boy foolish here, barred from my home.
I was fighting and robbing, doing drugs every day,
I was sent to the big house, for a very long stay.

Battered and bruised, naked in a cell,
Couldn't see past thirty, that's how far I fell.
I knew I had to change, it was not rocket science,
Reached out to Tabor Lodge, AA and Cork Alliance.
I enrolled in college, out in CIT,
To make a better life, for my family and me.
It took a few years, but I got my degree,
I'm not stupid after all, now the world can see.

I learned to read and write, at thirty-five years of age,
I had never read a book, never turned a single page.
So here I am, with a construction degree,
I'm going to start my own business, and help others like me.
Meditation helps me, to channel my rage,
Loving my life, since I turned a new page.
My wife is my hero, my kids are my life,
I'm happy at last, no more trouble and strife.

A good life is not a gift, in fact it's a right,
A house, a job, and a warm bed at night.
I hope my story, helps in some way,
No matter the obstacles, there is a better way.
I'm sorry if I hurt you, my apologies are sincere.
My name is Timmy Long, I hear you, I care.

Tracey

Tracey achieved a lot in her time,
A friend, a lover, a mother divine.
The good ones are always taken too soon,
She's lighting up the sky, brighter than the moon.
She had it tough, with no cribs or moans,
But boy did she suffer, from arthritis in her bones.
Then one day, out of the blue,
Tracey felt sick, she thought it was the flu.
As the pain got worse, she curled up in a ball,
Her family decided to give an ambulance a call.
She was so sick, she couldn't speak,
Day after day, week after week.
The family were worried, as to what they can do,
But truth be told, no one has a clue.
She never gave up, she fought the good fight,
But sepsis took control and quenched out her light.

The four amigos and Cardi b,
Liked to drink tea and some therapy.
Tracey, Sarah, Martina and Kim,
So close together, like sardines in a tin.
The pride and joy, for this queen bee,
Was handsome William and gorgeous Sophie.
To keep her centred and her mind on track,
She had bingo nights with Nanny Mac.
She had a wonderful family, they were all so great,
Thomas, James and sister Sinead.
No need to worry, for her children's fate,
Her sister Sinead stood up to the plate.
Her family are hurting, can't believe she's gone,
Especially poor Mary and her father Tom.
Tracey you were loved, more than you know,
It broke our hearts, that you had to go.

But know this, and this is from the heart,
When we all meet in heaven, we'll never be apart.

True Legend

So long John Caulfield, I wish you well,
The whole of Ireland, heard the rebel yell.
You took a team, that was on the floor,
Instilled belief, you made them soar.
In your first season, disaster beckoned,
Against the odds, you finished second.
The best thing you did, to get out of the mire,
You signed the great, Seani Maguire.

In 2016 you were on the rise,
You landed the cup, to no surprise.
In 2017 you filled us with pride,
The league and cup, were both on Leeside.
You won two cups, and a league title,
Three president cups, in front of Michael.
As a player you gave, your heart and soul,
A team player, who scored the odd goal.

All good things, come to an end,
From the bottom of my heart, I thank you my friend.
You gave us five years, the best we've had,
I'm city till I die, the good times and bad.
You leave us now, your head held high,
So sad to see you go, so hard to say goodbye.

In a way, you're a victim, of your own success,
No more will we settle, for second best.
You're a true Legend, at Cork City FC,
Your likes again, I don't think we'll see.
For one last time, the Cross should go barmy,
To salute Johnny C, and his Rebel Army.

Tweet For A Trial

The boy from Nigeria, is coming for a trial,
If nothing else, I admire his guile.
He could be like Messi, with magic feet,
Or the biggest con job, because of a tweet.
His name is Richard, and he likes McGregor,
Just like his hero, he's boxing clever.

When I was young, I had one dream,
To get a trial, with a professional team.
I trained so hard, I played my best,
I prayed at night, please give me a test.
I sent a tweet, to Cork City FC,
Please give me a trial, on the banks of the Lee.
In fairness to City, they didn't spin lines,
Just get it retweeted, 50,000 times.
Thank you God, and your mysterious ways,
I got all the tweets, at last happy days.

I'm off to Cork, my face is gleamin',
Thank you Decky Carey, and Damien Sreenan.
I promise you this, when I get my trial,
Your boss, Mr. Fenn, will have a huge smile.
You won't regret this, I know I will please ya,
Thank you, Mr. Chairman, for sorting my Visa.
I'll be the best, the league's ever seen,
Might even get a call up, for the boys in green.
I have nothing to offer, just my talent that's real,
But one day you'll make millions, with a mega transfer deal.

The Two Faced Liar

Evil shows in many forms,
Like spreading lies of new reforms.
I'll take back control, from the greedy elite,
I know them well, they live on my street.
I'll make them pay taxes, for the good of us all,
I'll protect you from invaders, by building a wall.
I'll build it so high, no one can get in,
Just give me your vote, to make sure that I win.

I've lied and cheated, with money on my mind,
I'm a two-faced liar, pretending to be kind.
I'll sell you dreams, that will never come true,
I'm destroying your world, and you don't have a clue.
The forests are burning, the ice sheets are melting,
But I'll turn a blind eye, 'cause the money's so tempting.

I'm a strong man, I'm a bully, I will always get my way,
Come along for the ride, on my private highway.
My most difficult foe, has been Covid 19,
Flowing all around us, an invisible stream.
I know it won't catch me, I'm up to the task,
I don't want to look weak, so I won't wear a mask.
The guy who works for you, don't you care if he suffers?
Not in the slightest, they're all losers and suckers.

I may be the chosen one, I think I'm immune,
The steroids maybe talking, have I spoken too soon.
My family's motto, is that might is right,
But I've a tickly cough, and my chest is quite tight.
I don't feel threatened, there's nothing can bring me down,
But Covid doesn't care if your bright, or just a clown.
The moral of this story, If you're a bully or a pariah,
They never see it coming, just like David and Goliath.

Ukraine A Nation Once Again

Vladimir Putin, the man with no soul,
To rule Ukraine, his ultimate goal.
Missiles and bombs rain down from the sky
We are liberating the people, is now the big lie.
Men, women, kids with teddy bears,
Fleeing, saying goodbye, in a river of tears.

We'll stop the bombing, we'll have a ceasefire,
Still bombing little children, thanks to Putin the liar.
Fair play to the EU, they opened their gates,
Took yachts and villas from Putin and his mates.
President Zelensky, the leader of Ukraine,
His mission in life, to cause Putin much pain.

He's holding his own, against the Russian Bear,
An inspiration to his people, not one ounce of fear.
The rest of the world, on the side of Ukraine,
Russia now covered in a massive black stain.
Millions of Ukrainians are fleeing to the West,
Pensioners and babies, for a well-deserved rest.

The only way this all ends,
Is a coup in the Kremlin, from Putin's close friends.
The Russian people are opening their eyes,
To Putin and his cronies, and their big fat lies.
We stand with Ukraine, we do what we can,
Sending nappies and medicines, In van after van.

The brave men and women, their lives they gave,
So that no Ukrainian, would be Putin's slave.
Let's isolate Russia, let's make their lives hell,
Till we hear the gong from the victory bell.
Thanks to the fighters, the brave women, the brave men,
Ukraine is at peace, a nation once again.

Live Life To The Full

For my wonderful grandchildren.

Don't listen to bluffers,
Wasters and chancers,
Seek out the singers,
Poets and dancers.

Don't stand on the corner,
Pay attention in school,
Live life to the full,
Be nobody's fool.

With thanks to:

My good friend Declan Carey, Chairman of FORAS and former Chairman of Cork City FC, for all his help to get this book to print. Top man!

Shane, Joe & Mairtín for all their help with editing and proofing the book.

Aaron Howey for the fantastic cover artwork and design.

Dermot Usher, owner of Cork City FC for his support in selling and distributing the books through the Cork City FC outlets and the wider fanbase.

My family - the inspiration for my poetry.

My wife and soulmate of 44 years Carol, our four wonderful sons. We are so proud of you, Anthony, Paul, Gary and Christopher.

Our eight amazing grandchildren Shay, Kuba, Dylan, Joey, Marley, Faye, Darragh and Emily.

To all the great friends I've made going to the Cross and beyond, too many to mention, but you know who you are! I genuinely value your friendship more than words can say.

City 'til I die,

Tony Tobin.

Credits

Author: Tony Tobin.
Foreword: Ken Tobin
Publisher, Compilation & Editing: Declan Carey.
Cover Art: Aaron Howey
Photographers: Doug Minihane, KBD Photos & Sportsfile
Co-editor: Shane O'Connor, Joe Leogue & Mairtín de Barra

ISBN: 9798868057441

Printed in Great Britain
by Amazon

32563774R00073